WERNER HOFMANN

IN TWENTIETH-

ART: *1890-1917*

TRANSLATED BY CHARLES KESSLER

ALLEN LANE—THE PENGUIN PRESS

LONDON 1969

First published in the U.S.A., 1969

First published in Great Britain, 1969

Allen Lane—The Penguin Press

Vigo Street, London W. 1

Copyright © George Braziller, Inc.

Designed by Jennie R. Bush

Printed in the U.S.A.

TURNING POINTS IN

TWENTIETH-CENTURY ART:

1890-1917

TURNING POINTS

CENTURY

CONTENTS

	Foreword	9
I	FINALE OR PRELUDE?	17
II	THE PIONEERS AND THEIR NINETEENTH-CENTURY BACKGROUND	27
III	NEGATIVE BEAUTY	71
IV	LAWFUL BEAUTY AND TRUTH TO LIFE	111
V	TOWARD THE ART OF ARTLESSNESS	195
VI	CONCLUSIONS	233
	Notes	243
	List of Artists	269
	Index	279

FOREWORD

here are problems whose challenge can haunt us, like a leitmotif, for years. We succumb to their attraction without at first gauging the consequences that flow from them. Some insignificant incident or a striking aphorism can in a flash reveal a thorny problem of which we are later unable to rid our minds. Frequently we forget the original occasion and do not recall it until our conscience sets out to trace prime causes.

In the winter of 1948 I spent some weeks at a rest center for European students. During this stay, I came across a well-thumbed issue of the *Partisan Review*, and read a contribution entitled "The Crisis of the Easel Picture." The author was the art critic Clement Greenberg. In time, title and contents of the short essay slipped from my memory, but not the problem it posed. I felt instinctively that the aphorism, "Crisis of the Easel Picture," spelled out a central, if not, indeed, the decisive, process in the art of our century. Since then I have tried to analyze, in a number of publications—most recently in *Grundlagen der modernen Kunst* (1966) (Foundations of Modern Art)—the origins, nature, and consequences of the problems involved. The present book picks up these same threads, but proposes a different perspective. Instead of showing the extensive links in art which subsist through the centuries, it marks the unobtrusive "small steps" taken by historical progress and concentrates on those shifts in emphasis which occurred between 1890 and 1917.

Symptoms of crisis in art, like every artistic manifestation of importance, make themselves felt before and after their time. Were it not so, the events concerned would lie unrelated in the lap of history, and we would have to content ourselves with the chronicle of their succession. If the easel picture is about to lose its predominant position we must ask: what are the forces that this crisis has released, when did they first appear, and what kind of art will this crisis produce?

The answers to the first two questions, so far as I am capable of giving them, can be found in the pages that follow. How very far they differ from the point of view expressed by Greenberg in 1948, I was able to establish when I reread his essay not long ago.[1] In 1948 he foresaw the development of action painting, a movement toward a new picture determined by the concepts of "all-over," "decentralized," and "polyphonic." Jackson Pollock, Mark Tobey, and others were quoted in confirmation.

For my part, I feel this answer is too restrictive. It is not so much that the easel picture and its conventions are in decline, as it is that Western painting as a whole appears to have come to the end of the ascendancy conferred on it by the Renaissance. This conjecture, not a death sentence but an affirmation of a loss of ground and prestige, can be substantiated by numerous symptoms. One of them I see in the fact that sculpture has recently emerged from under the shadow of painting. The publication in 1937 of Carola Giedion-Welcker's first comprehensive survey, *Modern Plastic Art* (rev. ed. *Contemporary Sculpture*, 1955) set off a new appreciation of plastic form that is far from finished. A parallel trend during the past twenty years and more has been the increasingly eager urge to put the third dimension to creative and inventive use. In the course of this trend, familiar categories, which had hitherto exercised binding authority, were transgressed.

[10]

Hybrids of painting and sculpture, sculpture and architecture, works of art and articles of everyday use are now innumerable. Neo-Dadaism, Nouveau Réalisme, Op Art, Pop Art, and most recently A-B-C Art (employing minimal spatial structures) furnish the proof.

These movements have given a radical twist to the "crisis" Greenberg observed in action painting. They have left the world of the "picture" behind, and in this way have established a contact between the present and the pioneering days of twentieth-century art, which is the subject of this book. It is not by chance that the panel picture's loss of prestige was accompanied by rediscovery of Jugendstil, Dada, De Stijl, and Constructivism.

What emerges is that the "crisis" was in its beginnings diagnosed on the one hand as a manifestation of decadence and on the other as an incentive to democratic renewal and a convalescence of art. In 1894 the artist and critic Henry van de Velde, in his lecture "Déblaiement d'Art" (Purification of Art), concluded that "the easel picture was simply a sign of hoary age, the slow evanescence of strength in an old man, the last moments of a dying one." This analysis was probably not unconnected with Albert Aurier's essay of 1891, "Le Symbolisme en Peinture," which stated: "The easel picture is nothing other than an illogical refinement invented to satisfy the imagination or commercial instinct of decadent cultures."[2] As early as 1825 the scholar Quatremère de Quincy had complained in his Girodet essay about the commercialization of painting whereby pictures, "designated by some people as void of any function," were produced without purpose. Delacroix's essay on Raphael, five years later, resumed this line of thought and held the panel picture's pride of place responsible for the progressive artistic decay since Raphael's age.

The masterpieces of painting and sculpture gradually became the objects of boastful luxury instead of stirring the soul or gratifying an intellectual craving, as in the time of Raphael. Painting confines itself more and more to easel pictures which are purely suited to being hung next to each other in galleries. We shall trace this disastrous evolution right down to the epoch of decay we have ourselves reached.[3]

If Delacroix regretted the Renaissance as the period when painters embellished temples and palaces for eternity and appealed to all, the painter Philipp Otto Runge, disgruntled by the art commercialism and "dam . . . building" of his contemporaries, pinned all his hopes on a "new architecture . . . more a continuation of Gothic than Greek," and created for the purpose of providing his pictures with a permanent home.

Thus artists have been aware for considerable time that the easel picture is not the final, most momentous word in European painting, let alone art as a whole. Art theory, however, has stubbornly declined to ponder this state of affairs, to pluck positive aspects out of the easel picture's crisis, and to recognize it for what it is—a process of creative liberation likely to prove as great as that of the events set in motion by the development of the easel picture in the late Middle Ages and the Renaissance.

For as long as we discuss the art of our own century in terms of painting, sculpture, and architecture—the autonomous creative categories established as orthodox in the Renaissance—we are not coming to grips with the basic problems. Similarly we shall miss the point if, like Hegel, we continue to regard "inwardness" and subjectivity as the most urgent representational components in "romantic art" and consequently concede the lead to painting. These attitudes are out of date, seeking, as they do, to prop the art of this century with arguments which perpetrate its falsification. That can only be proved by invalidating the clichés about the evolution of twentieth-century art. The alleged superiority of painting is a mere assumption. Nothing is more misleading than the point of view focused on the internal development of easel painting from Gauguin, Van Gogh, and Cézanne to, say, Soulages and de Staël. And the whole talk about "abstraction" as a new creative principle emphasizes a "moving away" from conventional concepts without stressing the enlarged reality which results from the interpenetration of two- and three-dimensional media of expression. To understand this new creative ubiquity as the key problem of twentieth-century art, the following pages propose a study of the ambiguity of Jugendstil,[4] a reappraisal of Cubism as having been the bridge in the development of creative consciousness whose crossing led to Dada and De Stijl—two movements which will be examined in their dialectically mutual relationship —and, finally, from the position reached, a fresh look at the situation at the turn of the century. This study aims not to record a complete calendar of events, but to make clear the essential lines of transition.

I

FINALE OR PRELUDE?

that group of pictorial concepts which, in contrast to the quiescent Earthly Paradise exempt from all change, interprets man's destiny as a journey or series of gradations. This ancient theme of the ages of man, incarnating birth and death as an endless sequence, was highly congenial to the pessimistic outlook and transitory form-language on the part of the Symbolists. It is a *memento mori* met in pictures by Munch, Hodler, and Klimt, and indeed in the decorative arts too. In 1892 Georges Lacombe produced four wood carvings for a bed, whose subjects were as follows: *The Dream, Birth of Man, The Uniting, The Death of Man.*[13] Without any doubt the theme's most intense formulation can be seen in Gauguin's *Where Do We Come From? What Are We? Where Are We Going?* (1897). That is the same question Picasso puts forward in *The End of the Road* and, a few years later, with incomparably greater restraint but the more impressively for that, in *La Vie (Ill. 32).* The circumspectly flowing contour which describes the seated pair is ambivalent. While merging man and woman indivisibly—analogous to Munch *(Ill. 30)* and Klimt *(Ill. 6)*—it is likewise in a position to partition off the individual in the loneliness of his broodings. There is no escape, whether for the pair or the solitary one, from this *cloisonné* of destiny. The three figures belong to a sphere of reality different from those standing in the foreground. The latter have a molded corporeality, and the effect of the former is one of engraved mottoes or fading memorials. Picasso, before deciding to lodge these mottoes in a transparent cube, let them make an appearance in a "picture within a picture." A preliminary sketch for *La Vie* hints at an easel on which can be seen a picture of the seated pair. It has been remarked, quite properly, that "the device of placing pictures within a picture has a suggestion of the collage technique of the Cubist period."[14]

Les Demoiselles d'Avignon (Ill. 33) constitutes an important link between *La Vie* and the *papiers collés (Ill. 97).* The provocatively crude handling of forms drowns at a first glance the allegorical content of the picture. This, curiously enough, burgeoned into dramatic intensity only during the actual process of production. The initial sketches had an impersonal, almost idyllic tinge: Picasso envisaged a sailor surrounded by five nude women and a second seaman, skull in hand, who would complement the group (*Ill. 34*). The concept evolved into three women with two apparently masked figures, recalling memories of the hybrid creatures of classical myth. Perhaps it is a manner of a votive offering or a paraphrase of the judgment of Paris (the fruit still life could be an indication of that), or a Diana bathing and accompanied by two satyrs, or the antithesis between man and woman, or the dualism between vitality and the threat of death.[15]

The yoke upon the differing degrees of reality has now acquired a brutal edge. Our gaze is made to pass abruptly from pictorial zones of near-reality to ones further removed. The top layer treatment sometimes seems final, at others sketchy and provisional. In parts the contours are sharp and cutting, then again hesitant and uncertain. Sometimes certain prominent details—heads, hands —emerge clearly, whereas other portions do not crystallize into any kind of cohesiveness, neither corporeal nor surface-like. The woman on the left is an example. Her body is transmogrified into a sort of drapery and looks as though it were sprouting out of a stiffly angular robe. Often the brittle, translucent interstices give an impression of being more spatial (therefore more intensively three-dimensional) than do the flat human shapes. The relationship between "figure" and "ground" attains ambiguity since figure, as in Jugendstil, forfeits its predominant role. The stratification of the spheres of reality, circumspectly intimated in *La Vie*, is given dramatic quality in *Les Demoiselles d'Avignon*, by means of an archaic mode of form expression in which the stiff, hard lineation is a harbinger of the analytical Cubism soon to set in (*Ills. 33, 96, 97*).

The attitude of the Expressionists toward the encounter between the sexes was completely enigmatic and saddled with problems. For them, separation and union, resignation and fulfillment, seem to follow upon one another with the inevitability of night upon day. Kirchner and Kokoschka first dealt with this theme in their cyclical works dating from the days of Jugendstil.

In 1904 Ernst Ludwig Kirchner completed his woodcut cycle *Man and Woman* (*Ill. 36*), a secularized history of the Creation which suggests comparison with Max Klinger's series of etchings—especially *Amor and Psyche* (1880). *Encounter* inspires *Abduction* (*Rape*) and is intensified to *Union*, then the lovers stand defenseless *Facing the World*, after which *Temptation* comes between them and leads to *Separation*. The fourth sheet is the one most clearly permeated by Jugendstil elements. The depiction of the figures "finds a symbolic linear equivalent on the left side of the print in the abstract forms suggesting dance movements and a group of staring eyes."[16]

These abstract forms are the beginning of the idiom which Kirchner, turned Expressionist, subsequently designated as his "hieroglyphic script." By this he meant not some firmly established scheme, but lines and forms that would reflect everything which manifests itself in the physical and intellectual sight of the artist: "Feeling constantly inspires fresh hieroglyphs which sort themselves out from the apparently confused initial mass of lines and practically assume the character of geometric signs."[17]

In the *Man and Woman* cycle this geometrization is still the medium for decorative, planar, and curvilinear elements; later Kirchner makes use of stiff, jagged, harshly contrasting form complexes (*Ill. 37*). This, in the light of stylistic criteria, represents in the truest sense of the word a breach—and yet, both the brittle "hieroglyphic script" of the artist's Expressionist period and the flowing line of his early woodcut cycle are guided by the same expressive principle.

The same applies to the contents. The *Man and Woman* cycle forms a bridge from the past to the future inasmuch as it

[35]

comprises all the principal concepts of Symbolism on which the iconography of the Expressionists is sustained: ugliness as demonic menace, the individual and the hostile crowd, woman as temptress, union and conflict of the sexes, the yearning for primordial vitality, *and* escape to elemental, paradisial conditions.

Reading the first sentence of the program of the Die Brücke group, written in 1906, it is probably not out of line to catch an echo of the claim by Kirchner and his friends that they are not simply the perpetuators of the artistic and ideological aspirations of Jugendstil, at that time in its final phase, but its radical regenerators: "With faith in progress, in a generation of creators as well as epicures, our summons is to youth everywhere, and like the youth with whom the future rests our aim is to obtain elbow-room and space to breathe amidst the entrenched older forces." Something, too, of the Jugendstil ardor of a Van de Velde lingers in the resolution, proclaimed in 1913, to fight "for a humane civilization which is the foundation of all real civilization."[18]

Kokoschka's pictorial narrative *Dreaming Youths* (*Ill. 38*) takes a less explicit course than does Kirchner's cycle. It appeared in 1908 under the imprint of the Wiener Werkstätte, whose director was Josef Hoffmann. The book's dedication left no question as to the source of his artistic inspiration: "For Gustav Klimt—in veneration." The pubescent, Gothicized figures in this tale are reminiscent of the tumblers and harlequins of Picasso's rose and blue periods and could stem just as well from the race of George Minne's striplings (*Ill. 39*). Their concentration focuses entirely on their own actions, or they abide passively in a weary *cloisonné* that seems equally to shelter and to engulf their fragility. Kokoschka's poetry conjures up the keynote of the loneliness that follows inexorably on fleeting unions:

> it is strange around me
> someone should answer
> everything follows its own trail.[19]

[36]

The yearning for a partner, because it seeks to comprise too much, finds no stepping-stone:

> and I reeled
> in the recognition of my flesh
> and was all-loving
> in my speech to a maid.[20]

The boundless, all-embracing craving for love changes to resignation and flees into an ivory tower *cloisonné* of constraint and seclusion. In these unredeemed tensions, incited by lusts, temptations, and trespasses—from which Kokoschka will soon break away (*Ill. 85*)—the spiritual ambiguity of Expressionism can be traced. Compared to this capacity for sado-masochistic suffering Matisse's *Joie de Vivre* (*Ill. 7*) seems ingenuously pagan.

Dreaming Youths manifests the existentialist mooring of Expressionism which Kokoschka will later define as a "message from self to fellow human."[21] When six years later he painted *The Wind's Bride (Tempest)* (*Ill. 41*), the idealized glorification of his love for Alma Mahler, he thawed out the self-absorption of cloisonnism and let the lovers coalesce with a vast terrestrial scene. This picture gave a baroque turn to one of the central themes of Symbolism: the unification of lovers. The spatial animation of *Tempest*—part ocean-breakers, part cloud-world—is reminiscent of the two integrative cloud formations of Van Gogh's *Starry Night* (*Ill. 9*). The comparison is less bold than it appears: Convinced that color itself expresses something, Van Gogh took pains to lend vividness to the "love of two lovers" through the application of complementary colors.[22] In her memoirs, Alma Mahler denied the complementary relationship between man and woman. She writes that Kokoschka "painted me as clinging trustingly to him in rain and wind and mountainous seas—looking to him for help—and he, with despotic countenance, calming the waves by the force radiating from him. . . ."[23] If this interpretation is accepted, then the picture's inspiration could derive from Delacroix's *Death of Sardanapalus* (1827–1828).

The *fin de siècle* precedents for Kokoschka's motif were many. Hodler (*Ill. 40*), Munch (*Ill. 42*), Axel Gallen (*Ill. 43*)—who furnished, as it were, a figurative commentary on Van Gogh's *Starry Night*—Klimt (*Eternal Spring*, 1884) and Rodin (*Amor and Psyche*, before 1886) come to mind. The list of examples could be extended into the fields of architectural ornament and interior design, and into literature (Richard Dehmel, *Zwei Menschen*, 1903) and music (Arnold Schoenberg, *Verklärte Nacht*, 1899).

The way from *Tempest* to Dante's Paolo and Francesca, the earliest vision of entwined lovers, is circuitous. In Kokoschka's painting the lovers find foothold amidst the spray of the elements on something that may be regarded as a dramatically furrowed shell. Or is it an opened fruit, or perhaps a frayed calyx? This detail too has its source in the nineteenth century. The shell and the calyx are two "visual metaphors"[24] which were particularly pleasing to Jugendstil artists for the evocation of growth and security. Seen in that light, the initial inspiration for the lovers' embrace can be sought in a work by an artist who has only recently been interpreted as one of Jugendstil's precursors, William Blake's *The King and the Queen of the Fairies* (1787). It is a straight line from the figures lying in a calyx, who made their reappearance[25] on the cover of the 1880 one-volume edition of *The Life and Works of William Blake*, to Kokoschka's *Tempest* and Boccioni's *The Dream (Paolo and Francesca) (Ill. 44)*.

Dante distinguished Paolo and Francesca from the other lovelorn sinners in the second circle of hell by allowing the two souls —"who go together/And seem upon the wind to be so light"[26]—to give their own account of their moving story. Boccioni, by throwing their closely clinging forms into relief against the chaotic mass of the damned, can be said to portray an idealization of the pair. This treatment mirrors a bourgeois prejudice: the segregation of the chosen few from the crowd. In his somewhat earlier drawing,

Mob Gathered Around a Monument (*Ill. 45*), the implicit tension is heightened into conflict.

Here we touch on another set of themes. The man of parts who creates his own world, well above the masses, is one of the most popular symbolic figures among painters and poets at the turn of the century. Rodin does obeisance to him in the proudly towering contour of his *Monument to Balzac* (*Ill. 46*). His work *The Thinker* (1879–1900) is also among those prototypes who have to bear a Promethean fate. Toulouse-Lautrec's Moses has become one with Mount Sinai (*Ill. 47*), while Frank Kupka's etching *The Black Idol* (*Ill. 48*) is similarly enthroned in the gloom of unapproachability. Nietzsche invokes related concepts of an elite in *Thus Spoke Zarathustra* and the poem "From the High Mountains" ("I learnt to dwell, where none have dwelt . . ."). His Superman, who lays down his own laws of behavior, could have inspired Boccioni's drawing and has affinity with the exclusivity of outlook that sets Kirchner's pair apart from the yapping crowd (*Ill. 36*), while his "I have learnt to dwell, where none have dwelt . . ." could be inscribed over the entrance to the Palais Stoclet where a wealthy businessman had his Earthly Paradise made. It is not without significance that this retreat of beauty stands guarded by a tower with four watchmen.

Echoes of this prestige symbol, represented by the guarded tower, are encountered a few years later in the tower fantasies of Antonio Sant'Elia. Like other contemporary Italian architects, Sant'Elia, before becoming prominent as the architectonic exponent of Futurism, derived crucial stimuli from Viennese Secession architecture as represented by the group of Otto Wagner's pupils. His ideas—he made a great many drawings, but built practically nothing—demonstrate a peculiar discrepancy. His megalomaniac imagination envisions structures reminiscent of the sacred architecture of Egypt and the ancient Orient, the result being awe-inspiring monuments standing in splendid isolation and

[39]

inaccessible to the common man. Yet these precincts dedicated to estheticism often had important communal functions to fulfill, and their imposingly solemn lines served to conceal factories, power stations, aircraft workshops, or railway stations.

Behind not a few of these temple, tower, and mausoleum visions there lurks—and this is the other aspect—a dynamic urge to expand that would like to see them magnified into a widely dispersed and unending urban layout. This is their strongest signpost to the future, to our own times. To Sant'Elia a metropolis is an unbroken interpenetration of buildings and highways, and ebullient lines of motion (*Ills. 49–50*). He compares the *"modern city"* with an *"immensely tumultuous song, agile, mobile, dynamic in all its parts"* and the modern house to a *"gigantic machine."*[27]

In some degree the Palais Stoclet, too, displays this ambivalence of outlook. It emphasizes its gulf from the profane outer world, yet at the same time its open groundplan (*Ill. 51*), fitting easily into its allotted space and harmonizing with the garden, contradicts any ivory tower notion. Its architect, Josef Hoffman, moreover, deliberately repudiates one of the principles of authoritarian architecture—symmetrical articulation. These traits hint at the strangely opposing elements which commingle in Jugendstil. It veers between esthetic exclusivity and the demand that art shall be for everyman, just as at one moment it is all for pessimism on the heroic scale and at another for a Utopian positivity toward life. In 1898 the first issue of the Viennese Secession's publication, *Ver Sacrum*, proclaimed that the group recognized no difference between art for art's sake and applied art, art for the rich and art for the poor. "Art belongs to everyone." This declaration of principle can be traced back to Van de Velde who, in 1895, in his "Aperçus en vue d'une synthèse d'art" (General Observations on a Synthesis of Art), wrote, "We cannot allow a sunderance in art whose purpose is unilaterally to allot a higher place to *one* of its numerous forms of manifestation and possibilities of expres-

[40]

sion than to another."[28] Claims like this constitute the theoretical background to Matisse's remark that a painting should provoke from its viewer the same reaction as an armchair.

These latent tensions between aristocratic and democratic ideals of art come to the fore, with aggressive trenchancy and a tincture of anarchism, about 1910 in the ideology of the Italian Futurists. Treading in Nietzsche's footsteps, they despise the philistine; mock the moral and intellectual criteria of the middle classes; rebel against every sort of tradition and convention; cite Bergson's *élan vital* as their authority; extol the worker, the savage, the criminal, and the child; and demand an unreserved profession of faith in modern technological civilization.

"We want to re-enter life."[29] The Futurist program's point is an extension of Van de Velde's hope for a "real union between art and life," but life is now interpreted as a simmering chaos, a raging tumult, that will not let itself be righted, pacified, and given gloss by means of esthetic standards. The skepticism about the omnipotence of an esthetic take-over flouts the Jugendstil creed in the same measure as it owes a debt to it.

In 1909, Filippo Tommaso Marinetti wrote in the *Initial Manifesto of Futurism*: "a roaring motor-car is more beautiful than the *Victory of Samothrace*."[30] Van de Velde had already asserted in 1903 that the Greek theater at Syracuse evinced the same caliber of intellect as that which invented the electric bulb: "In this creation there were precisely the identical principles at work as our engineers observe in the construction of their machines, their structures, their ocean-going steamers."[31] A few years later he opined that only those susceptible to the beauty of machines could appreciate the perfect rhythm of the Parthenon.[32] The emphasis shifts: Van de Velde still underlined the equivalence of art and technology, the Futurists gave precedence to the latter. Granted that they are at one in placing museums on a par with cemeteries, Van de Velde nevertheless hoped that a civilization concerned

[41]

with collecting curios might without violence become a thing of the past,[33] whereas the Futurists make its destruction the inescapable condition for a fresh start.

Set fire to the library shelves! . . . Deviate the course of the canals to flood the cellars of the museums! . . . We stand upon the summit of the world and once more we cast our challenge to the stars![34]

So runs the last sentence of Marinetti's manifesto. Once more, exaltation to the *Zarathustra* level, as it stood at the turn of the century, is invoked, but when a little later the first Futurist pictures are painted, the artists descend from their Olympian heights and throw themselves head over heels into the hectic bustle of modern life. Cosmic visions here and there are reminders of Marinetti's "challenge" (*Ill. 52*) but most of the pictures draw attention to the strident vitality of metropolitan existence or the triumph of technology: *The City Rises, The Noise of the Street Penetrates the House, Speed of an Automobile + Lights, Dynamic Hieroglyphic of the Bal Tabarin (Ill. 57).*

The Futurists wanted to put everything in flux. As "hieroglyphic" they availed themselves of the zigzag and the undulating line, in other words, of the Cubist and Jugendstil modes of expression alike,[35] as comparison between Carlo Carrà's *The Swimmers (Ill. 53)* and Klimt's *Fischblut (Ill. 54)* shows. The pursuit of omnimobility leads to interpenetration of mass and space. And this form process too can be traced back to the turn of the century. Boccioni's *Development of a Bottle in Space (Ill. 58)* develops— without there being any direct relationship—the plastic spiral of motion in Hermann Obrist's *Sketch for a Monument (Ill. 55).* By means of a Cubistic dissection of form, he lends dynamism to the alternating interpenetration of mass and energy which Jugendstil artists saw as a simile for the urge toward release, that is, dematerialization. Between Boccioni and Obrist lies the sobering

[42]

passage of the "bridge of form" with whose characteristics the following chapter will be concerned.

So we are back to the concepts of tower and peak, though this time we experience the apogee at a different level of symbolism. The matter is now no longer that of a lonely proclamation for *Odi profanum vulgus*—the Brücke painters' title for their artistic logbook—but one of graphic metaphors for the collective destiny. At the tip of Obrist's spiral kneels an angel who receives the human beings at the end of their weary way. The affinity to Bartholomé's sepulchral monument and Picasso's *Redemption* is patent.

Rodin's projected *Tower of Work* (c. 1894–1897) also falls into this category. This symbolic counterpart to the *Gates of Hell* was functionally complemented by the towers of work erected at the same time by the Chicago school of architects in the form of office skyscrapers. The poet Rainer Maria Rilke described Rodin's project as follows: "A circular tower stands on a square, fairly roomy base; . . . the arches . . . wind like a spiral ribbon to the top where a sculptured cornice holds them together. The whole is crowned by two winged figures standing on a platform enclosed by the cornice." Inside the tower the spiral staircase leading to the top is accompanied by a fillet of relief-work. "Handicraft follows upon handicraft here, carpenters, masons, smiths—vocation upon vocation, as though carried along and up by a gigantic momentum. . . ."[36] Two winged genii, *Les Bénédictions*, recall the Cantos VIII and XV of Dante's *Purgatory*, probably the source of Obrist's inspiration for his monument too.[37]

In Munch's *Menschenberg* (Human Mountain) (*Ill. 56*) the problem of salvation undergoes secularization, that is, a shift in perspective from Dante to Nietzsche. This painter's initial response to the issue "Whither do we go?" was pessimistic; his lithograph *Funeral March* (*Ill. 26*) is reminiscent of Picasso (*Ill. 22*) and Bartholomé (*Ill. 31*). Its message may be inferred from the

[43]

Requiem of a poet with whom he was in close sympathy: "Over and above procreation and fructification, death and resurrection, amalgamation and isolation, my exalted, profound, majestic calm of sterility sits enthroned! . . . My mighty Olympian soul in its grandiosity and barrenness."[38] In *Menschenberg*, however, Munch accomplished a triumphant turnabout toward the forces of light; his upward striving mass of men culminates in the figure of the prophet who, on behalf of all, opens his arms to the sun. That achieves the transcendence of death through creative action which Rodin also may have had in mind with his *Tower of Work* and which in similar terms was the prophecy of Van de Velde, the impassioned optimist, at the end of his address on "Déblaiement d'Art":

The road that we take is the glittering, golden stream that the sun emblazons in the spacious ocean and it leads us to the prodigious, purgatorial pyre lit by the heavenly body at its every setting. Through this curtain of fire art must pass to cleanse and to free itself from the filth that has befouled it![39]

The desire to free art from filth comprises the hope of a purer, nobler world. Should the reality of here and now, with its gross materialism, deny the artist this "purification," then he can do nothing except turn his back on it. These and other postulates lead the ideological escapism of Jugendstil artists to the discovery of abstract art. A further source, starting with Gauguin and his circle, was meditation on the inherent properties of color and form. Gauguin was not content "to exalt color and simplify the form";[40] his wish was to fathom the symbolic capacity of this intensification. On January 14, 1885, he wrote to his friend Émile Schuffenecker: "There are noble tones and common ones, tranquil, consoling harmonies, others that excite you by their boldness. . . . There are noble lines that deceive. . . . The straight line leads to infinity, the curve limits creation."[41]

In the following year the art historian Heinrich Wölfflin,

without, of course, knowing of Gauguin and his reflections, condensed this insight into the generalization, "Every mood has its precise expression."[42] These discoveries—or, more properly, rediscoveries[43]—are among the most important pronouncements in the modern "will to art."[44] They were taken up by Maurice Denis in 1890 when he wrote about a Gauguin picture that the impression on the viewer "could hardly proceed from the motif or from the natural motifs represented, but from the representation itself, forms and coloration."[45] Five years later he defined Symbolism as the conviction "that there existed for every emotion, for every human thought, a plastic equivalent, a corresponding beauty."[46] Obviously the logical conclusion to this line of thought must be to proclaim the superfluity of pictorial subject matter, which explains why the Symbolists and Jugendstil artists were under constant temptation either to transcend reality or to operate at two levels of expression. Kirchner's woodcut cycle, *Man and Woman* (*Ill. 36*), provides a good example: the abstract border is intended to lend the subject symbolic significance, but it remains for the viewer to choose between the complementally expository alternatives—as in the picture by Pisanello (see Note 16).

Kirchner and other artists discussed so far employed plastic equivalents in the sense of emphasis, simplification, and monumentalism of their emotions or expressional intentions as communicated by subject matter. Others—Mondrian, Kupka, and Kandinsky—went further: they decided upon the gradual elimination of subject matter. The art historians call this momentous step the invention or discovery of Abstract Painting. The evolution in form ensuing from this resolve is best appreciated by recalling the Art Nouveau beginnings of these three painters.

Piet Mondrian, the Dutchman, painted his first pictures without material content in 1913: vertical and horizontal lines formed variously sized planar compartments. About the same time he wrote in his journal that while masculinity finds expression in the vertical direction, femininity is to be apprehended in the prostrate lines of the ocean, and the artist's privilege is to convey simultaneously the male and female principles.[47] His pictures (*Ills. 59–60*) and his own comments are indirectly in the line of succession to Gauguin's observations on straight and curved, upright and crooked lines.

Soon after Gauguin, the theoretician Charles Henry, basing his thought on Charles Blanc's *Grammaire des Arts du Dessin* (Fundamentals of the Art of Drawing) (1867), ascribed qualities of calm, balance, and wisdom to the horizontal line. It is remarkable that Blanc already beheld in lineation an agent of masculine spiritualization of form and defined color as a female creative agent.[48] In 1908 Adolf Loos, in all probability unaware of these French speculations about the expressive content of abstract lines, wrote in his essay "Ornament und Verbrechen" ("Ornament and Crime"): "The cross, the first ornament to be conceived, had erotic origins—a horizontal line: the recumbent woman. A vertical line: the man penetrating her."[49]

Before Mondrian confronted the male with the female principle—for instance, in his *Pier and Ocean* drawings of 1914—he depicted them functioning separately and still in the code or "disguise" of subject matter[50]: the male principle by way of towers and slender trees (*Ill. 70*), the female by dune landscapes. The pictures of towers and dune landscapes began in 1909, whereas the paintings of trees ranged parallel to the plane of the picture go back to the years around 1900. Mondrian's horizontalism (*Ill. 60*) stems from Van de Velde's proto-abstract vocabulary (*Ill. 61*), whereas his verticalism can be compared with Klimt's paintings of woods (*Ill. 62*), with Kupka's *Nocturne* of 1900 (*Ill. 73*) and Larionov's *Rain* (*Ill. 63*). These portrayals have in common a vertical-rhythmic articulation which simplifies the outward appearance of Nature and seeks to transform it into a composition of planes. Ferdinand Hodler, the first practitioner and theoretician of pictorial "parallelism," wrote in an essay of 1897:

[46]

But how do we see things? As a contrast between brightness and darkness, light and shade, as a variety of colors. And, finally, as a matter of the degree to which physical shapes are brought into lineal relief from one another. The numerous perpendicular lines create an effect of being like one single vertical mark or a flat surface.[51]

When Mondrian in his three-cornered dialogue, "Natural and Abstract Reality" (1919–1920), wrote that flatness gives a "much more intrinsic" appearance to things than their material manifestation permits, he was providing an *ex post facto* justification for the turn taken by his painting toward geometric Abstract Art. His few pictures of individuals afford important proof of that. In the triptych *Evolution* (*Ill. 65*) he made use of the full-face view—a familiar feature since Hodler and Munch[52]—and adapted the technique of parallelism to the human face. The work itself constitutes a notable link between Symbolism and Mondrian's abstract art. It reflects his preoccupation with theosophy and his debate with Jan Toorop, the most outstanding of the Dutch Art Nouveau artists, whom he met in 1908. The concept of the picture is presumably related to the three stages of womanhood, of which Munch gave his version in *The Dance of Life* (1899–1900) and in the lithograph *Woman* (*Ill. 66*).[53] Jan Toorop's *The Three Brides* (*Ill. 67*) may be surmised as the direct source of inspiration: "The three brides stand for the nun bride of Christ . . . the human, innocent, virgin bride . . . and the Bride of Satan. . . ."[54]

The interpretation to be placed on Mondrian's *Evolution* is not as straightforward as that, even though the geometric attributes of the three figures no doubt indicate how each of the women is meant to personify a different phase of consciousness. From the dialogue already cited we can infer where this evolution—and with it Mondrian's painting—will lead: "Man, in the eyes of cosmic evolution, progresses . . . from matter to spirit . . ."[55]

[47]

That renders Abstract Art the furthest point, inevitable and dictated by cosmic law, in the process of purgation foreseen by Van de Velde in his address of 1894 ("Déblaiement d'Art").

Leaving aside such external influences as the decisive stimuli imparted by the Cubists, with which we shall be concerned later, the stage attained in form by Mondrian around 1913–1914 (*Ill. 59*) represents a continuation of the "right angle" undercurrent in Jugendstil (*Ills. 17–20*). The occurrence of unexpected parallels between "applied" and "pure" abstraction in geometrical art at the turn of the century is attested to by the following comparison. In 1902 Josef Hoffmann—soon after 1900 he also saw the right angle as "fundamental to everything"[56]—executed a stucco relief for a door headpiece (*Ill. 18*). A decade later the Czech Frank Kupka, who had studied in Vienna but by that date had long resided in Paris, painted reliefs which are precise counterparts to Hoffmann's (*Ill. 68*). It is not impossible that Kupka received some impetus in the direction of his vertical planes through Edward Gordon Craig, whose transparent screens produced a revolution in stage design at the turn of the century (*Ill. 69*).[57] Without doubt Kupka's discovery of abstraction stems from his Art Nouveau phase. *Nocturne*, one of his first nonobjective canvases (*Ill. 71*), derives from the *Keyboard Landscape* (*Ill. 72*) and can be traced back to the floating parallelism of his *Nocturne* drawing of 1900 (*Ill. 73*).

Mondrian wrote: "Rectilinearity . . . signifies a 'consummation' of curvature in which the latter conforms more closely to nature."[58] Here, without being aware of it, he was in agreement with Gauguin, who had perceived in the curve a limitation on creativeness and in the straight line an expansion to infinity. Limitation would need to be comprehended as restriction to the sensual and material, the way of the straight line as a venture into the intangible zones of the pure spirit. Kupka's abstract works are based, on the one hand, on Jugendstil's vertical right-angled linearity, on the other, on its curving dilation of line. A juxtaposition

[48]

1. Josef Hoffmann, Palais Stoclet, Brussels, 1905–11.
2. Josef Hoffmann, Palais Stoclet, dining room, Brussels, 1905–11.

3. Henri Matisse, *Woman with the Hat*, 1905.

4. Georges Rouault, *M. et Mme. Poulot*, 1905.

5. Maurice Vlaminck, *La Partie de Campagne*, 1905.

3

4

5

[51]

6. Gustav Klimt, *The Kiss (Realization)*, dining room frieze, Palais Stoclet, Brussels, 1905–08.

7. Henri Matisse, *Joie de Vivre*, 1905–06.

7

8. Paul Gauguin, *Jacob Wrestling with the Angel (The Vision after the Sermon)*, 1888.

9. Vincent van Gogh, *Starry Night*, 1889.

10. Hector Guimard, Paris subway station (Métropolitain), entrance gate, c. 1900.

8

9

10

11. Anonymous, Entrance door, Milan, 1899.

12. August Endell, Atelier Elvira, facade (destroyed), Munich, 1897.

11

12

13. Bernhard Pankok, Drawing room, Munich, c. 1900.

14. Antonio Gaudí, Casa Batlló, interior, Barcelona, 1905–07.

15. Émile Gallé, Shell-shaped crystal bowl, 1899.
16. Victor Horta, Hotel van Eetveld, hall, Brussels, 1895.

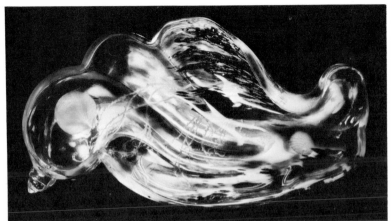

15

16

17. Adolf Loos, Haberdashery Shop Goldman (destroyed), Vienna, 1898.

18. Josef Hoffmann, Supraporte (stucco relief), Vienna, 1902.

19. Frank Lloyd Wright, Unity Church, ceiling detail, Oak Park, Illinois, 1906.

20. Otto Wagner, Postal Savings Bank, interior, Vienna, 1904–06.

21. Henri Matisse, *The Red Studio*, 1911.

20

21

22. Pablo Picasso, *The End of the Road (Redemption)*, c. 1898.

23. Eugen Kirchner, *November* (from *Pan*), 1896.

24. Otto Eckmann, Initial (designed for the Rudhard Type Foundry, Offenbach), c. 1900.

25. Odilon Redon, *La Mort Verte*, after 1905.

24

25

[63]

26. Edvard Munch, *Funeral March*, 1897.

27. Wassily Kandinsky, Catalogue jacket, *Der Blaue Reiter*, 1911.

of his *Amorpha, Fugue in Two Colors* (*Ill. 74*) with Van de Velde's *Abstract Composition* (*Ill. 75*) or the cosmic growth fantasies of Munich Jugendstil (*Ill. 76*) make this evident.[59] It is curious that Kupka, although living in Paris, should have ratified his conversion to Abstract Art in terms of Central European Jugendstil.

Matisse, we have heard, paves the way for Kandinsky's abstract paintings. The proposition may by and large be correct, but it needs qualification. During his stay in the Paris of 1906–1907, Kandinsky assuredly saw *Joie de Vivre,* yet the experience cannot be traced in his artistic development. Then and in succeeding years Kandinsky made less use of linear unisonance than Matisse who, after *Joie de Vivre*, often incurred the hazards of "arabesque pure" adventures.[60] In the years of his Munich apprenticeship (1896–1906), Kandinsky came into contact with Jugendstil—his biographer mentions his encounter with Hermann Obrist and Van de Velde[61]—and did indeed learn "to exalt color and simplify the form," but remained aloof from temptations to indulge in heady linearity to which Obrist, August Endell, and Schmithals were prone (*Ill. 76*). Although in pictures like *Couple Riding* (*Ill. 77*) it can be shown that Kandinsky, as regards the theme of the lovers and in the decorative planar rhythm, paid his respects to Jugendstil, it must not be overlooked that the mellow and gentle overall impression, conveying a peculiarly static and poised sensation, owes nothing to curvilinear reticulation. The dominant directional axes are missing; that is due to the discreet, mottled color application which derives from the dabbing, additive brush technique of the Neo-Impressionists, but is notably lacking in their systematism.[62] Certain traits, like the predilection for rich films of color and the slow unfolding of narrative, analogous to frieze-work, are reminiscent of Klimt. (Both participated in the 1904 Dresden Art Exhibition.)

The Russo-German romanticism of these wonderland scenes is on the one hand linked to the widespread, trite, chivalric versification at the turn of the century,[63] while on the other it presages the propensity to flee from reality and the urge toward a nobler and more beautiful, more primal and more elementary world, a world which will reject the subject's—in Mondrian's sense— "disguise." Even when he had turned to Abstract Art, the motif of chivalry did not relax its hold on Kandinsky: he painted a St. George (*Ill. 78*) and christened the group founded by himself and Franz Marc in 1911 Der Blaue Reiter.

Nevertheless, in setting out for fresh artistic shores, Kandinsky had to throw some of his previous luggage overboard, and that by way of abandoning the dreamy melancholy of his impressionistic pictures in favor of a fresh and turbulent impetus in his creative methods. He was probably alluding to this renunciation, which his Fauvist productions between 1906 and 1910 heralded, when in 1914 he referred retrospectively to perils which had at that period menaced his creativity. He mentioned, in the first place, "the danger of stylized form, which is either stillborn or dies of inanition" and in the second, "the danger of ornamental form, which in the main is the form of external beauty. . . ."[64] If this remark constitutes abjuration of the estheticism and universal unisonant relationships, from Gauguin's cloisonnism to Jugendstil, then another statement is no less clearly the opposite of what Symbolism and Art Nouveau wanted to achieve with plastic equivalents. Kandinsky said:

> It is no music that I seek to paint.
> It is no psychic state I seek to picture.[65]

Kandinsky's misgivings about the perils of stylized and ornamental form can be taken as having general application, for the spring of action for his decision—abandonment of the standard of form already attained—is common to all the artists discussed in this chapter. Although they are adjudged to be the pioneers of art in our century, consideration of their achievements in this direction has been "played down" in order to define initially their formal relationship to, and attitudes toward, Symbolism and Jugendstil.

The pioneer character of these personalities was the result of their resolve to call into question their own position and to seek out fresh realms of form lacking, as yet, conventional approval. This happened during the short span of years from 1905 to 1911.[66] And what is the nature of these new realms? Some intimations have been given. Matisse tautens curvilinearity or enriches it with contrapuntal facets (*Ill. 21*); Picasso breaches cloisonnism and extracts brittle, angular forms (*Ill. 33*); the Futurists upset Art Nouveau's flow of line with harsh staccato rhythms adopted from the Cubists; Kokoschka and Kirchner make use of coarser, more aggressive lines and cruder color contrasts; Mondrian learns how to handle the geometric asceticism of the Cubist mode of expression; and even Kupka turns to tenser, more austere forms that relinquish the lyricism of Jugendstil. Finally, Kandinsky disintegrates pictorial content into a seemingly chaotic *status nascendi*.

Discontent comes to the fore everywhere during these years; doubts become clamant about the exclusive validity of the cultivated and established pattern of form, the ingratiatingly glad tidings of Jugendstil are accused of superficiality, the appeal of matured form positions is undermined and efforts are made to reveal novel *elementary* means of utterance. The movement of protest is directed against that formal rhetoric for which Maurice Denis, in 1908, coined the contemptuous phrase about the "pretentious facility of the improvisers of Art Nouveau."[67] It is also, of course, directed against the neo-traditionalist solutions Denis had in mind in making his criticism. Matisse wrote in the same year in his "Notes d'un Peintre": "The simplest means are those which enable an artist to express himself best."[68]

The Fauves were the first to risk a novel elementariness of form and color. Their example caught on and incited the discovery within a few years of further, still more radical realms of

[67]

elementary expression that were subsequently labeled Cubism, Expressionism, Futurism, geometric and dramatic Abstract Art. But, once more, the common factor among these artists who assign themselves the task of venturing into unknown territory is that, surmounting or even denying their own beginnings, they abjure the formal consensus of Art Nouveau, renounce the *facilité* of curvilinearity, and attempt "to unlearn," to throw aside routine, in order to press forward into the wilderness of new, unfamiliar encounters with form.

Fascinated by the ideal of primordiality and absolute truthfulness, it is an outlook that seeks to recover lost artlessness by artful means, that is, a conscious exercise of will. That the course they took was problematic must not be disguised, but it was not unprecedented either. Sir Joshua Reynolds had described it in his *Discourses*:

> I cannot help suspecting, that in this instance the ancients had an easier task than the moderns. They had, probably, little or nothing to unlearn, as their manners were nearly approaching to this desirable simplicity; while the modern artist, before he can see the truth of things, is obliged to remove a veil, with which the fashion of the times thought proper to cover her.[69]

III

NEGATIVE BEAUTY

peaking of "the simplest means," Matisse had in mind an articulation different from that of Kokoschka, Kandinsky, or Mondrian. The bridge of form, from whose passage the artists mentioned previously anticipated a fresh directness and primordiality of expression, was crossed at not one, but several points. The pitch of the new primary forms varied accordingly. Ranging from grimacing lampoon and coarse cubification to the staid discipline imposed by compass and ruler, their scope stretched from barbarism and primitiveness to immaculate geometric form complexes. Appreciation of this holds the key to the background of events which set in motion the reorientation of form that began about 1905.

The moment has now come to take into consideration those rigid, brittle, geometric forms of the *fin de siècle* noted earlier: on the one hand, the bulky rusticality of Van Gogh, the bold and massive contours of Gauguin, the stiff-limbed figures of Cézanne; on the other, the sober rectangularity used by architects and designers like Charles Rennie Mackintosh, Otto Wagner, Josef Hoffmann, Frank Lloyd Wright, and—in particularly explicit manner—Adolf Loos to vent their resistance to curvilinearity. This aspect is indispensable to an analysis of the occurrences around 1905, because it shows how the effort to harden and tauten the handling

[71]

of form stretched in two opposing directions. There was experimentation at one end with an expressive coarsening and distortion, at the other, with attainment of a geometric abstraction of reality. Nevertheless, these trends, before they parted company and constituted themselves into Expressionism and Cubism, did for a short while adopt a common approach.

Among the influences assimilated by Picasso in *Les Demoiselles d'Avignon (Ill. 33)*—a work that stands halfway between Expressionism and Cubism—are those of primitive Iberian sculptures, African masks, and El Greco. This painting reflects, moreover, the challenge presented by Cézanne's *The Large Bathers (Ill. 79)* and Matisse's *Joie de Vivre (Ill. 7)*. To these formal sources should be added another. Probably Picasso visited the great retrospective Gauguin exhibition of 1906 in the Salon d'Automne which included such important paintings as *Jacob Wrestling With the Angel* (1888), *The Yellow Christ* (1889), and the wood relief *Soyez Amoureuses* (c. 1889). They presented a rudimentary, mythical picture of Man that was in glaring contrast to the latter-day refinement of European civilization. Here was an artist trying to recover for art its magical and, hence, original haunts and thereby to invoke the aid of unknown life forces. The barbarism of Gauguin's *formes rudimentaires* must have fortified Picasso in his aims to the same degree as did the artistic accomplishments of the primitive races who—discovered and extolled by Gauguin a decade earlier—had, around 1905, once again impinged on the consciousness of the avant-garde. A wooden sculpture of 1907 by Picasso testifies to that.[1]

In the year of *Les Demoiselles d'Avignon*, another creation also served to document this deliberately primitive *genre*: Derain's *Squatting Man (Ill. 80)* is the faithful cubification of a broodingly squatting posture often utilized by Gauguin, the first time in *Vineyard in Arles with Breton Women* (1880)—an example, incidentally, of a blend between several spheres of reality—and subsequently in the catalogue for the Café Volpini exhibition.[2] A trace of this concept can still be perceived in Matisse's *Dance* (*Ill. 81*). Derain's squatting figure, one of modern sculpture's incunabula, is an archaizing answer to both Rodin's form liquefaction and Maillol's harmoniously balanced corporeal fullness (*Ill. 82*),[3] an answer amounting to derision of anatomy as it had dominated European criteria of beauty since the Renaissance. A year later Brancusi similarly abandoned the human figure to the Cubist stoniness of sculpted block (*Ill. 83*).

In 1907 a Gauguin exhibition took place in Vienna. Was it the source of inspiration for the barbaric eroticism displayed by the youthful Kokoschka in the drawings for his drama *Murder Is the Hope of Women* (*Ill. 84*), performed for the first time in 1909? The assumption is a fair one. The animal in the background is an erotic allegory often employed by Gauguin, whose recumbent women have a way of reverting from depth to surface, in the direction of the viewer, that is akin to Kokoschka's reclining figure.[4] The factors of conflict and the insulting, aggressive brutality of deformation are new. The gentle cloisonnism of *Dreaming Youths* (*Ill. 38*) is shattered, and melancholy restraint is transformed into brute ferocity.[5] It is an advance—a first proclamation, in modern eyes, of the Theater of Cruelty—which corresponds to the turning point reached by Picasso between *La Vie* and *Les Demoiselles d'Avignon*. In his self-portrait bust of 1908 Kokoschka uses aggressive colors to obtain the magic spell of horrifying grimace (*Ill. 85*).

Similar symptoms of form are also encountered whenever an artist does not fall back on the mythical prototype of Primeval Man but—in succession to Van Gogh—looks at the world around him. Emil Nolde's *Peasants* (*Ill. 86*) may be in the line of Van Gogh's figures, but lack their God-fearing, simple humanity. Wild contortions have transformed their bodies and have stamped their features with the reflection of visionary frenzies. Behind this weird convulsion lies a presentiment of the stifling, crushing corporeality that fetters mankind.

Also held in bond and defiled by their instincts are those

people whom the artists discovered among the scum of mass society in the border reaches of metropolitan existence. They stimulate the artist by their barbarous vitality. To express the aggressive brutality of a barmaid, Maurice Vlaminck uses the devices of caricature (*Ill. 88*), whereas Michael Larionov transforms a prostitute into a devouring grotesque idol (*Ill. 87*). In the Salon d'Automne in 1905, Georges Rouault exhibited a triptych which caused a scandal. The three panels were entitled *M. et Mme. Poulot* (*Ill. 4*; after Léon Bloy's *The Poor Woman*),[6] *Prostitute*, and *Terpsichore*. The Parisians were outraged, morally and esthetically, for Rouault's figures held up a mirror to the hypocrisy of middle-class society, which saw itself reflected with repulsive distortion. These were specters stepping out of Stygian zones beyond the capacity of Art Nouveau and Jugendstil to master. And these misshapen, inert, impotent lumps of flesh are foreshadowed by Gauguin too, as in the woodcut *Personnages Comiques* that he made in 1899 for his periodical *Le Sourire* (*Ill. 89*).

These examples, taken from the perspective of barbarized form, demonstrate how dissonance replaces consonance, calm and harmoniously balanced planes are supplanted by broken ones, and form abandons its flow of line in favor of coarse unruliness, crystalline rigidity, or ponderous blockishness. The most vivid description of this change of attitude is to be found in a letter, dated May 3, 1929, by Kirchner.[7] Here he contrasts two types of line and says that, while he loves one, the other makes him feel "almost uneasy" (*Ill. 90*). It was consistent with this option for an incisive, angular articulation that the Expressionist Kirchner should have disavowed his early work, the *Man and Woman* cycle.[8]

Picasso's reaction to the curvilinearity, as he would have us understand it, prevalent at the turn of the century, is quoted in Françoise Gilot's memoir:

We were all Modern-Style artists. There were so many wild,

delirious curves in those subway entrances and in all other Modern-Style manifestations, that I, even though I limited myself almost exclusively to straight lines, was participating in my fashion in the Modern-Style movement. Because even if you are against a movement, you're still part of it.

Picasso's remark, if correctly recorded, seems to confirm our initially advanced premise or to postulate a nexus between Art Nouveau and its "subjugators": "The pro and the con are, after all, two aspects of the same movement."[9]

The selection of new forms, which Kirchner dissected into its rudimentary components, soon faced artists with the quandary of freedom of choice. Reducing the matter to simplest terms they had to decide between two possibilities: should they aim at the largest feasible variety of fresh characters or hieroglyphs, or should they resolve on a limited cipher? In the answer lies the parting of the ways between the Expressionists and the Cubists. The insistence of the former on immediacy shorn of all trappings logically directed them into the realms of proemial form and thus, in the last resort, along the path toward those primary devices that pledged them to no common factor and created the impression of chaos emanating from Kandinsky's first abstract watercolor (*Ill. 91*).

At Paris, preference was given to limitation and codification rather than expansion. This route began with the attempt of Matisse to confine the new mode of expression to a dialogue between straight lines and curves and ended with the still more restrictive verdict by the Cubists and Mondrian on behalf of the straight line. In 1908 Matisse said to his students, "Do remember that a curved line is more easily and securely established in its character by contrast with the straight one which so often accompanies it. The same may be said of the straight line. If you see all forms as being round, they lose all character."[10] These admonitions reveal a self-critical awareness which aims to see the light, gliding lineation of *Joie de Vivre* idiomatically enriched by more energetic expressions of form. The result can be perceived in the subtle counterpoint of *The Red Studio* (*Ill. 21*) which depends on the contrast between straight and rounded lines. Yet the duologue, rather than culminating in conflict, tapers off evenly; this is the harbinger of a new, systematic quest for beauty and harmony with which Matisse after 1908 strives to imbue the international circle of his *Académie* pupils.

These principles of form, however surprising their enunciation by a Fauve, were anything but new. They are to be found, for example, in Walter Crane's *Line and Form* (1900), a treatise dating from Jugendstil days. Crane felt that sharp or very violent contrasts could have destructive effects.[11] By sanctioning two systems for his textbook reader—the oval and the rectangular— Crane affirmed allegiance to the two basic forms of Jugendstil, curvilinearity and the right angle, and Matisse's approved pair of contrasts. His advice, though, did not tend toward underlining the antitheses between lines and curves but to the amelioration of these contrasting elements, if not indeed to a plea for the uniform. He has no bias, attaches equal importance to either system of approach (*Ill. 92*), and opines, "We can accustom ourselves to any method," for each is a deliberate abstract of perceptual data, an artistic ideogram.[12]

The issue of free choice not only held the attention of the author of a theory of graphic art, but also caused a certain hesitation on the part of artists who at the time sought to codify the new means of expression in practical terms. Should they employ oval or rectangular form cells, opt for organic or cubic rhythms? The preliminary studies for *Joie de Vivre* (*Ill. 35*) and *Les Demoiselles d'Avignon* (*Ill. 34*) illustrate the issue. Straight lines are dominant in Matisse's sketch, and to try to find the curvilinearity which lends the final version of the picture a flowing, mellow character is a vain endeavor. One of Picasso's earliest drafts, on the other hand, consists entirely of well-rounded convex curves that subsequently assume more and more pointed, angular shapes. Only in the ultimate phases of their formative process do Matisse and Picasso decide which system to adhere to, the one to the oval, the other to the rectangular. Admittedly, it must not be overlooked that, unlike Walter Crane, neither painter felt bound to the conventional image of human anatomy. Their articulation of form could not but shock their contemporaries since it declined to be kept in tutelage by empiric facts and proclaimed autonomy from them.

In 1907 not only Picasso, but Braque too, opted in favor of the straight line. It signified the supersession of the Fauves and the initiation of what has probably been the most momentous art movement of this century: Cubism. Georges Braque, briefly a Fauve—"Matisse and Derain showed me the way," he later remarked[13]—in that year painted a number of landscapes whose sequence leaves no doubt about the shift in emphasis. One of them (*Ill. 93*) is still reminiscent of the curvilinear background setting to Matisse's *Joie de Vivre* (*Ill. 7*), and curvilinearity is their "figured bass."[14] During that same year Braque produced the first of several L'Estaque landscapes (*Ill. 94*). Angles and broken planes are its dominant features. The well of Nature seems petrified; its buds do not open but are forced into cubification. The rhythm of organic growth has been supplanted by harsh immutability.

In the following year, when Braque's landscapes in this *genre* were rejected by the Salon d'Automne, Matisse is supposed to have exclaimed impatiently, *"Toujours les cubes,"* "thereby helping to familiarize the word which was soon to develop into Cubism."[15] The source of Matisse's irritation, the new form language's abandonment of counterpoint for uniformity, is probably precisely what Braque had in mind. Cubism's "monotonous" strain, its almost exclusive reliance on straight lines, is the result of its ambition to simplify the polymorphism of the physical world and to impose rigor and discipline on pictorial expression. That involved renunciation of the voluntary absence of rules among the Fauves. If Cubism is seen as a process of form codification, then it

[77]

must be said that Braque's 1907 landscape went further in that direction than did Picasso's contemporary pictures. With one reservation: *Les Demoiselles d'Avignon* was not a fully realized example of early Cubist discipline, but the prototype for a subsequent, more complex stage in Cubism—the interpenetration of different strata of reality.

At the time when Braque was painting his L'Estaque landscapes and Picasso *Les Demoiselles d'Avignon*, a new lodestar rose over the Parisian avant-garde world—Paul Cézanne. He played an important role in the geometric codification of the new form literals. This contention rests on the occurrence of two art gallery events in 1907—the Cézanne Memorial Exhibition in the Salon d'Automne, and the display of seventy-nine of his watercolors at Bernheim-Jeune (*Ill. 95*)—and the publication of "Souvenirs sur Paul Cézanne et lettres inédites" (Recollections of Paul Cézanne and [His] Unedited Letters) by Émile Bernard in October, 1907, in the *Mercure de France*. This publication included the dictum, "Everything in nature is modelled on the sphere, the cone and the cylinder. It is necessary to teach one's self to paint with these simple forms, one will then be able to do all that one wants."[16]

Did the Cubists adhere to these axioms? Reading what Daniel-Henry Kahnweiler, eyewitness and chronicler of the birth of Cubism, says on the subject is like listening to Cézanne's own voice: "You must start with objects of the simplest sort. With cylindrical tree-trunks and square houses, in the case of a landscape, with plates, symmetrical receptacles, round fruits in a still life."[17] The incipient Cubists had to unlearn their accustomed modes of expression and, so to speak, take their place in the classroom alongside the drawing student on whom Walter Crane had impressed in 1900,

The cube and the sphere, the ellipse, the cone, and the pyramid . . . present themselves to the student as elementary tests of draughtsmanship. . . . Such forms being more simple and regular than any natural forms, they are supposed to reduce the problem of drawing to its simplest conditions.[18]

What was new about the Cubists' endeavors was not that they took a geometric interpenetration of reality for their frame of reference, but the way that they handled it. Crane's didactic Cubism—with its string of antecedents[19]—sought to begin from a geometrically figured bass of reality, to give solidity to patterns and to clothe bones with flesh. The Cubists, however, were not—according to Kahnweiler—concerned merely with attaining a convenient pattern for transcription of reality, but wanted to detect "proto-lines" and so to lay bare aspects of the inner structure of the perceptual world. Another point of difference was that the Cubists made no attempt to distinguish objectively the details of their geometric idiom. Crane still felt himself bound by the rules of perspective and anatomy. The Cubists ignored illusionist content and objective intelligibility. Instead they concentrated on the highest possible degree of coherent construction among the pictorial elements. Their point of departure was the urge to achieve greater firmness and structure in the expression of form, an urge in opposition to both Jugendstil and Fauvist practice. Cézanne, undoubtedly, contributed to an involution of the objective content of paintings through his later work, which lacked perspective and often clarity of purpose, as well as probably promoting the tendency toward rigidity and archaism in portrayal of the human form. And in relation to the Cubist interpenetration of faceted, transparent color planes, the poet Guillaume Apollinaire could say with justice, "Cézanne's last pictures and his water-colors belong to cubism. . . ."[20] (*Ill. 95*).

Around 1907–1908 Cézanne's influence overshadowed that of Gauguin and Van Gogh, while simultaneously the Fauves had to relinquish leadership of the avant-garde to the Cubists. That meant transition from the first phase of rejuvenation in form, an expressively sensual one, to a second phase which drew its inspiration from straight lines. The Cubists themselves rarely allowed rectilinearity a completely paramount place. That development was left to a painter who raised the antisensualist asceticism of "Analytical Cubism" (*Ill. 96*) to the perfection of geometric purism and the extreme triumph of straight line and right angle: Piet Mondrian. At this juncture, the evolution of painting attained a purity and absoluteness of form that challenges comparison with the geometric trends at the turn of the century. (We will see later where the differences lie.) The gain in vigor yielded by Mondrian's restriction of the formal vocabulary to a minimum may be set alongside the structural principle of Horatian diction lauded by Nietzsche in *Götzen-Dämmerung* (Twilight of the Idols):

This mosaic of words, where each radiates its efficacy as an element of euphony, location, and concept to right and to left and over the whole, this minimum in volume and number of intimations, this maximum in vigour of intimations obtained thereby— all that is Roman and, if my assessment is acceptable, refinement of the most pre-eminent kind. All the rest of poetry becomes in contrast a shade too vulgar—sheer subjective chatter.

Whether this characterizes Horace's specifically "Roman" quality is a moot point, but Nietzsche undoubtedly caught the accent of patrician restraint and ascetic criterion of style which also distinguishes Mondrian and his circle from the effusive intemperance of those who ostensibly paint with the spontaneity of birds singing their song.[21]

It may be that the ascetic impulse which determined the trend of Cubism's beginnings and Mondrian's crucial decisions can best be defined in a phrase that takes us back to the start of the century. In 1901 Van de Velde sang the praises of the "negative beauty" of English furniture and *objets d'art*. For him their succinct beauty lay in "what they did not, what they no longer have"—the deliberate display of ornament.[22] Abandonment of nonfunctional "titil-

28. Edvard Munch, *The Cry*, 1895.

29. Edvard Munch, *Portrait of Friedrich Nietzsche*, 1906.

30. Edvard Munch, *The Kiss*, 1892.

31. Paul Albert Bartholomé, *Monument to the Dead*, 1899.

32. Pablo Picasso, *La Vie*, 1903.

31

32

33. Pablo Picasso, *Les Demoiselles d'Avignon*, 1907.

34. Pablo Picasso, *Les Demoiselles d'Avignon*, studies, 1907.

35. Henri Matisse, *Joie de Vivre*, sketch, 1905.

34

35

[85]

36. Ernst Ludwig Kirchner, *Man and Woman*, woodcut cycle, 1904.

1. Encounter

4. Facing the World

2. Abduction (Rape)

5. Temptation

3. Union

6. Separation

37. Ernst Ludwig Kirchner, *Streetwalkers by a Shop Window*, 1913.

38. Oskar Kokoschka, *Dreaming Youths*, 1908.

39. Georges Minne, *Kneeling Youth*, c. 1898.

40. Ferdinand Hodler, *Night*, 1890.

38

39

40

41. Oskar Kokoschka, *The Wind's Bride (Tempest)*, 1914.

42. Edvard Munch, *Meeting in Infinity (Encounter in Space)*, 1899.

43. Axel Gallen, Vignette (from *Pan*), 1895.

41

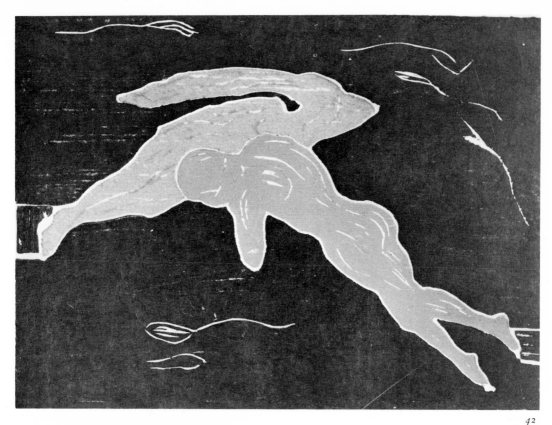

42

43

44

15

44. Umberto Boccioni, *The Dream (Paolo and Francesca),* 1908.
45. Umberto Boccioni, *Mob Gathered Around a Monument,* 1908.

46. Auguste Rodin, *Monument to Balzac*, 1897.

[93]

47. Henri de Toulouse-Lautrec, *Au Pied du Sinai*, book jacket, 1898.

48. Frank Kupka, *The Black Idol*, 1900.

47

48

49. Antonio Sant'Elia, *"New City,"* study, 1914.

50. Antonio Sant'Elia, *Lighthouse Tower*, 1913.

49

50

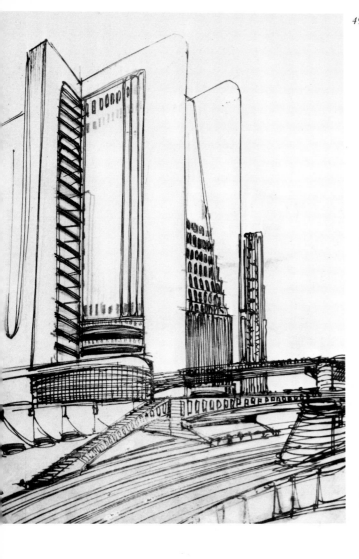

51. Josef Hoffmann, Palais Stoclet, site plan, Brussels, 1905–11.

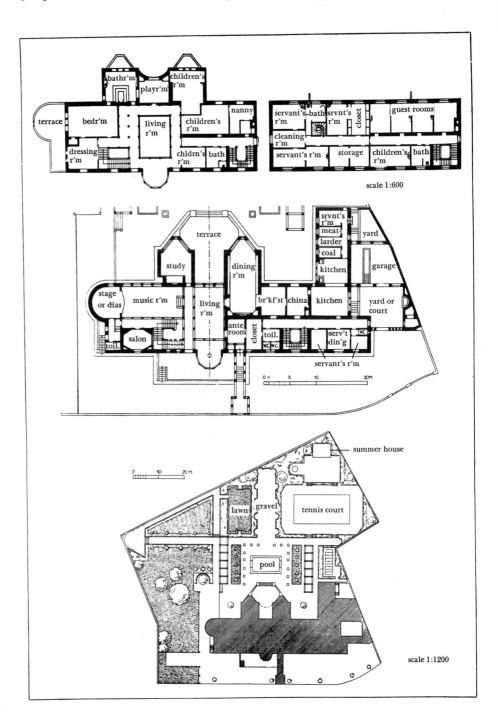

scale 1:600

scale 1:1200

lation of the senses" is a hallmark of the geometrical purist variety of Jugendstil, a plea for the smooth surface and unadorned cube. Ornamentation, dispensable because detachable, is denounced as a luxury and one which disguises the probity of form and its functional requirements. That expresses a point of view stemming not only from the strictness of puritanical antisensualism but also from a propensity for elegant understatement that knows how to extract from restraint a "negative" beauty more eloquent than its positive counterpart. "Heard melodies are sweet, but those unheard/Are sweeter. . . ." (Keats).

As long ago as 1849 Ruskin demanded that it should be a "general law . . . not to decorate things belonging to purposes of active and occupied life," adding, "Wherever you can rest, there decorate," though "You must not mix ornament with business." The enunciation of such principles rendered Ruskin the champion of the "negative," artless beauty of utilitarian objects. That was why he denounced the nonfunctional decoration of railway stations and the "bad habit of trying to disguise disagreeable necessities by some form of sudden decoration."[23] This stricture held good not only for mid-nineteenth-century abuses but equally applied to the weak point of decorative exuberance with which the ornamental-curvilinear school of Jugendstil was decades later to make a show.

Another Cassandra was at hand. In 1892 Louis H. Sullivan wrote that "it would be greatly for our esthetic good if we should refrain entirely from the use of ornament for a period of years, in order that our thought might concentrate acutely upon the production of buildings well formed and comely in the nude." He extolled "the great volume of unadorned masses" and claimed that architects should become well grounded in pure and simple forms.[24] Sullivan himself never took ornamental abstinence as far as his pupil Frank Lloyd Wright who, in the case of buildings and utilitarian objects alike, put into practice his teacher's stipulations. Wright's Unity Church (*Ills. 19, 98*) is an example of strict

[97]

conformation, within and without, to the principle of structural rectangularity. As a form of "figured bass" it does not hesitate to harness to its own purposes the surge of line transmitted by ornamentation itself. The effect is no longer that of appliqué, and therefore detachable, but of tectonic accentuation, and as such legitimized by need. His revolving office chair (*Ill. 99*) demonstrates the exercise of productive austerity and simplicity in the field of furniture which thereby acquires tectonic character.

The first European to familiarize himself with what was happening in America, give support, and try to propagate these ideas in the Old World was the Viennese architect Adolf Loos. From 1893 to 1896 he stayed in the United States, mainly in New York, Philadelphia, and Chicago, and probably had read Sullivan's essay, "Ornament in Architecture." His own rejection of ornament was first aired in a publication of 1898.[25] That same year saw the building of his men's-wear shop, Goldman and Salatsch, in Vienna (*Ill. 17*). Incensed by that section of the Viennese Secession—and by Josef Maria Olbrich in particular—which wallowed in ornamentation, Loos's attitude became a phobia. In his pamphlet "Ornament und Verbrechen" (1908) he formulated his repudiation in aggressive, intolerant, cutting terms which owed their vehemence to a state of moral indignation. "The evolution of culture is synonymous with the elimination of ornamentation from utilitarian objects." Anyone in the twentieth century "smearing walls with erotic symbols is a degenerate or a criminal."[26]

Had Loos been no more than an advocate of "unadorned masses" and "pure and simple forms" (Sullivan), his niche in history would be alongside Mackintosh (*Ill. 100*), Wagner (*Ill. 20*), Wright (*Ill. 99*), and Hoffmann (*Ill. 18*), that is, in the circle of those who, metaphorically speaking, resolved to adopt the "rectangular method" and stood up for this conviction in their buildings and interior decorations. Loos was not, however, a mere contemner of ornamentation. For him, ornament was merely one

[98]

symptom of an esthetic inflation induced by Jugendstil which, masquerading as "artistic totality," had obtruded on the world of utilitarian objects. He derided the monopolistic lust of the architect or designer who appointed himself an all-powerful dictator, and fancied himself ordained to give everything the stamp of creative interpretation. Loos pronounced a veto on the artist's usurpation of the craftsman's functions and his right to design chairs, lighting fixtures, baths, ashtrays, and even ties, or, in other words, to imbue with lyrical qualities everyday utensils and to impose esthetic criteria upon them.

Loos's historical significance lies in his repudiation, formulated with a brilliance equal to the superiority of his arguments, of the claim to overall domination of design put forward by the "total artist." Thereby he became the preacher of a "negative beauty," going far beyond what Van de Velde, whose opinions he attacked, understood by that phrase.[27] Whereas his artistic philosophy also derived from the renunciation of self-conscious beautification preached by some of his contemporaries in the Jugendstil world, Loos trod the panestheticism of "artistic totality" underfoot and championed heterogeneity in the place of homogeneity. He rebelled against the vision of the future seen by Van de Velde in the following terms: "The time will come when we shall refuse to live in a room in which not every single object proclaims the common will to create but one single emotional impact."[28] In 1900, prior to Van de Velde's publication of these notions, Loos caricatured esthetic conformism in his *Von einem armen reichen Mann* (Story of a Poor Rich Man)—another sort of King Midas:

The architect had meant well with him. He had thought of everything. The teeniest of receptacles had a place precisely prepared for it. It was a comfortable home, but not without headaches, and that was why during the first few weeks the architect supervised the domesticity so that no mistake should creep in. The rich man did his best. All the same it did happen that he put away a book and, his thoughts elsewhere, pushed it into a

[99]

rack meant for newspapers. Or else that he tipped his cigar-ash into the table-recess intended to house the lighter. Once an object had been lifted from its place, there was no end to the amount of guesswork and research required to reinstate it correctly, and sometimes the architect had to unfurl his detailed plans to rediscover a match-box's position.[29]

Loos did not arrogate to himself the status of an esthetic Grand Inquisitor. His stringency was directed at the products of the Secession arts and crafts trade. For the rest, he was content to leave it to those who dwelt in the rooms created by him how they should furnish them and what works of art they should purchase to stand wherever it best pleased them. A somewhat major restriction admittedly impinged on this freedom of action because Loos frequently made furniture and walls into a single unit, lending them a structural character which did not allow for their transferability. And often enough the walls displayed deliberately sunk panels for pictures. Loos the practitioner was not always at one with Loos the theoretician.[30] Nevertheless it can be said of his interiors that, compared with those of Olbrich and Hoffmann, the framework does not encroach upon the content. They lack the sacrosanct and immovable solemnity of the artistic totality aiming at a single emotional impact; they offer multifarious transitions from the work of art to the anonymous cabinetmaker's products, and from the ordinary utensil to the architectonic framework. The "negative beauty" this enemy of ornament had in mind was not the beauty of forbearance but one, plural in character, distributed over various though coexistent planes of reality.

To the degree that Loos liberated artistic achievement from indiscriminate intercourse with utilitarian objects and, analagously, in the spirit of Ruskin postulated a clean cut between "architecture" and "mere building" (in the light of which only mausoleums and monuments may lay any claim to being works of art),[31] he restored to artistic creation the dignity of a purpose of its own. At the same time, he freed the remaining realms of re-

[100]

ality from the esthetic dictatorship of the "total artist" and allowed them to regain their inherent quality. His attitude represents, therefore, the proclamation of two points: the emancipation of the individual, the "poor rich man," and the emancipation of material "things" from the esthetic straitjacket of Jugendstil.

In Loos's outlook, emancipation of the individual is linked with a moral protest which, in matters of form, raises its voice against both the consistent palliation of life and the hypocritical illusion of the harmonious idyll. At the beginning of the century Loos prophesied the coming revolt of instinctive and multiple vitality against complete domination by beauty and unison. His poor rich man ends as prisoner of beauty and opines, "Now it's a matter of learning how to handle your own ashes." Loos, in unmistakable terms and far ahead of the Expressionists, the Futurists, and the Dadaists, denounced the pseudoreality of the esthetic mausoleum in the name of life and its spontaneous forces when he turned on the world of art and exclaimed, "Show us how birth and death, the agonized cries of an injured son, the death-rattle in the throat of a mother, the final thoughts of a daughter seeking her own death happen and look in a bed-room designed by Olbrich."[32]

When Loos flung this challenge at his fellow artists in 1903, there was scarcely anyone prepared to accept it. Some years were to pass before these same artists set out to destroy both the untarnished luster of the Jugendstil world and its supersession by an unruly, enigmatic reality which took no account of moderation nor paid deference to morality or so-called good taste. That is the socially critical aspect of the artistic brutalism first given formal expression by Picasso, Kokoschka, Larionov, and Rouault and which but a few years later was to erupt anew in the antibourgeois attitude of the Futurists and Dadaists.

The discovery that there are aspects of life for which the assonant and concordant rule of Jugendstil expression is no match, and dissatisfaction with interiors whose entire contents were only capable of producing a single emotional impact, were apprehensions that served also to throw a new light on man-made objects. Suddenly, they were once more embodiments of a vital diversity whose charm lay precisely in that its workings could not be retraced to one uniform "figured bass." The "total artist" was irritated by the sight of an interior in which "there is no connecting link, where a thousand elements jostle and contradict each other and testify to the flightiness of mind and abundance of inconsistencies among those whose taste has here prevailed."[33] Against this view Loos put forward an avowal of a reality which shuns esthetic window dressing. Its hallmark is the lack of common measure. What this architect who wanted to be known only as a master builder—that in itself is symptomatic of a harking back to the "elementary"—had to say about these matters heralded the revelation of those fragmentary, fortuitous realms of reality which would shortly be discovered by the Cubists with their collages and would eventually lead to an extreme of "negative beauty"— Marcel Duchamp's "ready-mades" (*Ills. 104–105*)—at the opposite pole to Mondrian's "negative beauty." At this point genuine reality not only rebuts every effort at esthetic integration but is shown, without the tutelary intervention of composition, quite simply as it is. In the ready-made, reality is displayed without the mask of form, and the "ideal," which the mask sought to superimpose, has served its turn. Everyday, trivial objects are declared in their utterly artless ordinariness and banality to be full-fledged. It would be all too easy to dismiss Duchamp's notion of submitting a urinal for exhibition as intent "to dumbfound the bourgeois." It is probably nearer the psychological mark to recall Nietzsche's words: "He who finally becomes aware how long and how thoroughly he has been fooled will be ready to embrace even the ugliest of reality in consolation."[34]

It may be taken for granted that the line of thought leading from Loos, the contemner of ornamentation, to Duchamp, the contemner of art, does not fail to come in contact with the aspirations of the Cubists. How close the connection was between the Viennese architect, as theoretician and practitioner, and the work of Picasso and Braque is disclosed by applying the criterion of "coexistence of differing degrees of reality" to his own production.

The Steiner House, built by Loos in a Viennese villa suburb, was—until its vandalistic maltreatment some years ago—a Cubist architectonic creation of the first rank. This claim rests only partially on the strength of the smooth, provocatively unadorned sobriety of the house's garden front (*Ill. 101*) from whose strict symmetry fifteen rectangular openings have been excised. Dispensing with framework profiles, and thus esthetic "setting," these apertures have an element of abruptness which is still further enhanced by their apparently arbitrary dimensions. The cube's flat top has an air of suddenness, and the absence of cornice and roof underlines the bareness of the homogeneous mural mass, which gives the impression of having been sliced out of a larger cube.

To appreciate the Cubist qualities of the house it is necessary to compare the garden front with the street front (*Ill. 102*). The first point to be noticed is that these two principal fronts have nothing in common. It is impossible to draw any conclusions from the one about the other—they could belong to different buildings. The only point of meeting between them is at the narrow lateral front (*Ill. 103*) where they breed a hybrid whose marks can be ascribed in part to this, in part to that main front. If the side facing the garden follows a rigidly rectilineal design, the excessively steep downward slope of the roof's camber on the other gives priority to the curving plane.[35] Each is operative at a different level of reality. The garden front is cool and dispassionate, but of immaculate, elegant austerity. The roof, which would interfere with this purity of planar relationships, has been squeezed away to the street front which is not, as might have been expected, "representative" but in form and material makes an impression not far removed from the commonplace and the vulgar. This pro-

[103]

vocative contrast between absolute and relative forms, of temperate geometry with brute substance, is a reminder that Loos did not shrink from allowing various levels of reality to coexist inside his houses also.

At the same time, a similar dialectical device was practiced in the analytical phase of Cubism. Intimations of material objects lurked in isolated dispersal, amidst geometric "proto-lines": here the fragment of a violin, there a bottle label or a hint at facial lineaments.

This coexistence between different levels of reality had the following background. In their efforts to lend their paintings two planes of reality, an idealistic and an actual one, the Cubists hit on the technique of the *trompe-l'oeil*:

In the summer [1910], which he again spends in Estaque, Braque is able to take the introduction of "actual objects"—that is to say, painted things simulating nature and brought into the picture without deformation or discoloration—a step further. Letters are for the first time found in a *Guitar Player* of this period. Lyrical painting at this juncture rediscovered a new world of beauty which slept unobserved in the wall-posters, shop-windows, and sign-boards, and which play such a big part today in our visual impressions.[36]

Shortly afterwards yet another, decisive step is taken. The painted illusion is replaced by the collage, the real reality of colored strips of paper, newspaper, oilcloth, glass, and sawdust (*Ill. 97*). The collage confronts the abstract reality of the artistic signs with the tangible world of everyday facts—they enhance each other reciprocally. Kahnweiler's advice to the viewer was to integrate the two pictorial poles into a single, completely assimilated production:

For by reason of "actual" details of this kind being lodged in

[104]

the picture, the imagination is goaded and flickers of recollection attach themselves which proceed to piece together in the mind the finished object from the "actual" stimulus and the pattern of form. The desired corporeal representation thus ensues in its entirety in the consciousness of the observer.[37]

While these experiments were taking place in the seclusion of a few Parisian studios, in Munich Kandinsky was pondering ideas that resemble a theoretical commentary on them. The Cubists had barely decided to link different degrees of reality when Kandinsky diagnosed the structural "characteristic of a great intellectual epoch" as lying in plurality of form and materials. Kandinsky's far-sightedness enabled him to make a correct analysis: this process of composition had consequences that opened a new chapter in the history of European art.

Kandinsky's essay "Über die Formfrage" ("On the Question of Form"), written in 1911, contains the statement that contemporary art "has at its disposal the whole storeroom, that is to say, *every material*, from the 'hardest' to the simply two-dimensionally existent (or abstract), finds application as a form element."[38]

It is understood that Kandinsky could not, at the time of writing, have been familiar with the Parisian collages. His sources of inspiration for this premise of an antithetical choice of materials—grand realism and grand abstraction—have to be assumed as coming from elsewhere.[39] Perhaps his reading of Wilhelm Worringer's *Abstraktion und Einfühlung (Abstraction and Empathy)* had sharpened his discernment for the perception of polarities of form and the potentialities of extremes. Worringer's much-discussed disquisition was issued in 1908 by the same publisher who in 1912 brought out the Blaue Reiter almanac which also contained Kandinsky's above-quoted essay. It is known that Worringer's theories caused great stir among the Blaue Reiter group and that there was talk of inviting this "splendid mind" to contribute to the planned second volume of the almanac.[40] In a dialectical simplification Worringer compared and contrasted the imitative instinct and the urge toward abstraction, according recognition to the latter as the effort "to remove the individual thing from the external world's arbitrariness and apparent fortuitousness and to perpetuate it through an approach to abstract forms."[41]

Worringer based himself on Alois Riegl, the Viennese art historian, and to make a just assessment of the share of art theory in establishing the new "negative beauty" it is necessary to begin with him. Riegl's main work, *Die spätrömische Kunstindustrie* (Late Roman Craft Industry), was published in 1901 and consisted of an investigation into the "internal artistic character" of the late period in heathen antiquity which at that time was generally in disrepute as an epoch of barbaric decay.[42] His point of departure bore an affinity to that of Jugendstil insofar as he condemned the disdain for craftsmanship and the patronage bestowed on the allegedly "higher," and consequently differently principled, figurative art. Riegl maintained that one and the same "will to art" is to be perceived in all artistic accomplishments and he set out to rehabilitate, that is, to effect a positive revaluation of the form characteristics of late Antiquity—lack of vital beauty, massiness, inarticulation of contours, an inflexibly crystalline adherence to rules. The cardinal point of his argument, cited subsequently by Worringer, was an analysis of the late Classical reliefs on the Arch of Constantine in Rome. In his view they demonstrate —at this point Van de Velde's "negative beauty" (1901) should be borne in mind—"a different sort of beauty . . . which may be termed crystalline because it constitutes the primary and most everlasting law of form for inanimate material and is that relatively closest to absolute beauty (substantial individuality), though this is admittedly only capable of being conceived."[43] Riegl granted that art of this sort made intellectual demands on an observer and could not therefore "impossibly count any longer on general approbation, not even that of all educated contemporaries."[44] Memory of the consternation on the part of initial visitors to the Cubist and Expressionist exhibitions involuntarily comes to mind.

[106]

Riegl was not content to affirm on late Roman art's behalf a positive "will to art" aiming at strict symmetry. His Hegelian outlook launched him into trying to identify within this "will to art" a dialectical thesis and antithesis. In the course of this effort he met with a pair of opposites that is already familiar from Cubist practice: remote and imminent reality. An observer looking at the reliefs on the Arch of Constantine, thought Riegl, will be struck on the one hand by the trend toward "highest disciplined beauty," and on the other, while viewing the rows of stereotype figures from a distance, by an impression of extreme vitality deriving from the "lively alternation of light and shade." From this he concluded

that both aims in all branches of the fine arts—beauty and life-likeness—were in the case of the Constantinian reliefs just as much a point of aspiration and attainment too as in Classic art. Whereas there [i.e., in Classic art] they fused in a harmonious compromise (vital beauty), in this instance they have once more diverged to their respective extremes—in the one case towards highest disciplined beauty in strict crystalloid form, in the other towards life-likeness in its most extreme shape of momentary optic effect.[45]

This passage was quoted by Worringer. It is a fair assumption that it exercised a decisive influence on Kandinsky's speculations regarding the future of modern art or contributed substantially to the dialectical aspects of his thoughts on the subject. Riegl's claim for late Antiquity respecting the polarity of the two "aims in all branches of the fine arts" was simultaneously a description of the poles to which Kandinsky ten years later assigned the "corporeal forms torn out of the storeroom of material"—grand abstraction and grand realism. In the same way that Riegl construed the situation of late Antiquity as a fracture of the Classical synthesis of form in vital beauty, so Kandinsky interpreted the duality of grand abstraction and grand realism as the decomposition product of the "vital beauty" which from the Renaissance until the end of the nineteenth century had held sway as the highest ideal of European art. "These two elements," Kandinsky asserted,

have always been present in art, being labelled "purely artistic" and "objective." The first found expression in the second, whereby the second served the first. It was a matter of heterogeneous balance which apparently sought to attain the apex of the ideal in absolute equilibrium. And it would seem that this ideal today no longer represents an aim, that the lever operating the scales has disappeared, and that its two pans propose to lead a separate existence as individual, independent units.

He added the following commentary on the ensuing dichotomy:

On the one hand abstraction will be deprived of its excursive support in the objective sphere and the observer will feel the ground falling from under his feet. It will be said, "Art is losing its hold." On the other hand the objective sphere will be deprived of the excursive idealization provided by abstract art (the "artistic" element) and the observer will feel himself nailed to the floor. It will be said, "Art is losing its ideal."[46]

A few years later, between 1913 and 1914, Kandinsky's diagnosis was confirmed by the facts. The two planes of reality which had still been united in the Cubist collages parted company. Mondrian's geometrization rejects the fragmentary sprinklings of reality and works out the system of "proto-lines" to a degree of idealist immaculateness (*Ill. 107*); Marcel Duchamp radicalized what began with the Cubists' arbitrary newspaper cuttings—the mere display and unartistic presentation of actual reality (*Ills. 104–105*). The situation is one that can be described in Riegl's terms: "disciplined beauty" and "life-likeness" mark themselves off into separate spheres.

IV

LAWFUL BEAUTY AND TRUTH TO LIFE

To strike an interim balance, let us recapitulate: Around 1905–1906 Matisse and his circle stood at the forefront of the European avant-garde. It was they who released the Fauvist tidal wave which was soon to strike Central and Eastern Europe. At Dresden, quite independently of what was happening at Paris, Ernst Ludwig Kirchner, Erich Heckel, Karl Schmidt-Rottluff, and Fritz Bleyl founded Die Brücke in 1905, the artist group from which German Expressionism evolved. In Vienna the Kunstschau presented its first exhibition in 1908. As "principal madcap,"[1] Oskar Kokoschka, twenty-two at the time, attracted mainly hostile attention. Strangely enough, Richard Gerstl, the most genuine Viennese Fauve (*Ill. 109*) was not represented. A consistent outsider who preferred the company of the composer Arnold Schoenberg and his associates to that of his fellow painters, he committed suicide a few months before the Kunstschau opening. At Munich Kandinsky, with his Russian compatriot Alexei von Jawlensky and Gabriele Münter, founded the Neue Künstlervereinigung (New Artists' Union) in 1909. Like his friends, he was passing through his Fauvist phase. In Russia itself the avant-garde, although striking out on its own, kept in constant touch with Matisse.[2]

In Paris the Fauves were being outstripped by the Cubists. Between 1908 and 1910 they were considered the most advanced modernist movement. Dissemination, reinterpretation, and imitation of their creative principles abroad did not lag far behind. In Germany and Italy, not to mention the effects of Cubism on Paris-domiciled painters, faceted planes and sharp-edged masses began to be copied at the start of the century's second decade.

Yet, at this same stage, sights were being trained on positions so novel as to render Cubist probings downright traditional. Between 1910 and 1913 the earliest examples of "abstract art" were produced: Kandinsky, Larionov, Kupka, Delaunay, and Mondrian painted pictures containing no hint of the world of familiar experience (*see Ills. 60, 74, 91, 111, 120*).[3] Regarded as the proceedings of a revolutionary character inaugurating a fresh epoch in European art, these works took to its extreme conclusion Maurice Denis' contention that "a picture—before being a war-horse, a nude, or any sort of story—is essentially a flat surface with a layer of colors assembled in a certain order."[4] This argument had been promulgated in 1890 as a theoretical vindication of Synthetism and has been quoted to satiety ever since. Kandinsky, by denying a picture any "digressive dependence on subject matter" and authorizing the painter to elevate the "purely artistic" factor to the status of an autarchic value, in theory and in practice endowed the autonomy of the *fait pictural*, proclaimed by Denis and reinforced by the Fauves and the Cubists, with supremacy. Thus it is possible to trace a straight line from Gauguin via Matisse to Kandinsky.

Whereas this logical sequence—deriving not from the *Zeitgeist*, but from the positions assumed by the artists who occasioned it—is indubitable, it illuminates only *one* aspect of Kandinsky's historical significance. The other is no less important. His proclamation, as a theorist, of the new "grand realism" not only gave new license to the depictions of objects, as against those formalist theories which had subordinated them to the primacy of form and color, but let the "purely artistic" factor appear *expendable.* He sanctioned the painter's "expulsion from a picture of the super-

52. Giacomo Balla, *Mercury Passing Before the Sun*, 1914.

53

54

53. Carlo Carrà, *The Swimmers*, 1910.
54. Gustav Klimt, *Fischblut* (Apathy), 1903.

55. Hermann Obrist, *Sketch for a Monument*, c. 1902.

56. Edvard Munch, *Menschenberg* (Human Mountain), sketch, 1910.

55

56

[115]

57. Gino Severini, *Dynamic Hieroglyphic of the Bal Tabarin*, 1912.

58. Umberto Boccioni, *Development of a Bottle in Space*, 1912.

57

58

59. Piet Mondrian, *Composition in Oval (Composition in Blue, Grey, and Pink)*, 1913–14.

60. Piet Mondrian, *Pier and Ocean*, 1914.

61. Henry van de Velde, *Sun at Ocean (Rhythmic Synthesis)*, c. 1888–89.

60

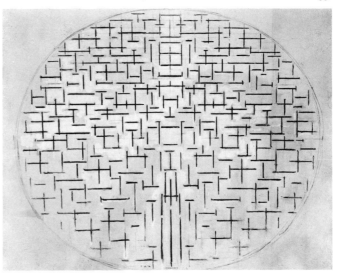

59

61

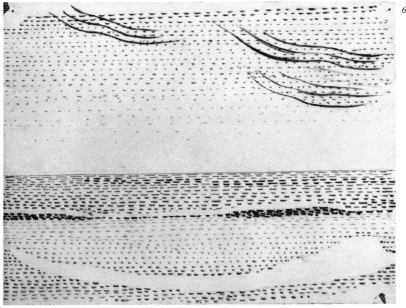

[117]

62

63

62. Gustav Klimt, *Woods*, c. 1900.

63. Michael Larionov, *Rain*, 1902.

64. Piet Mondrian, *Composition with Trees II*, 1912–13.

64

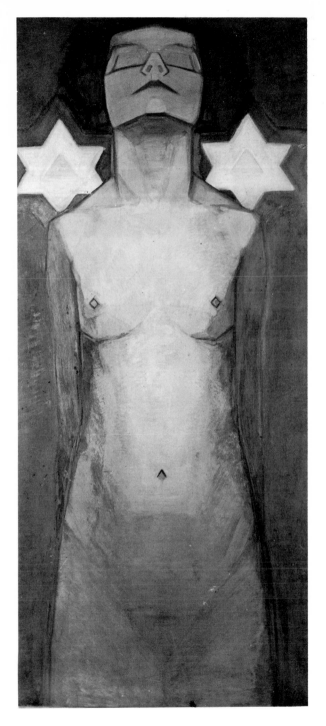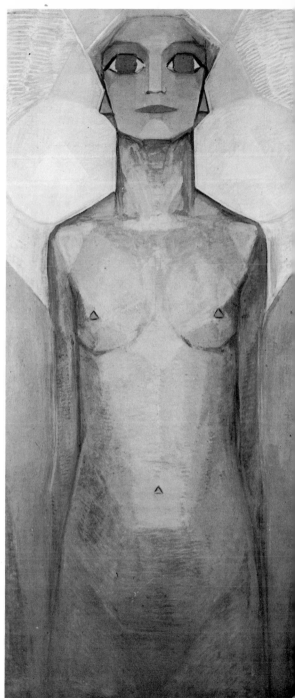

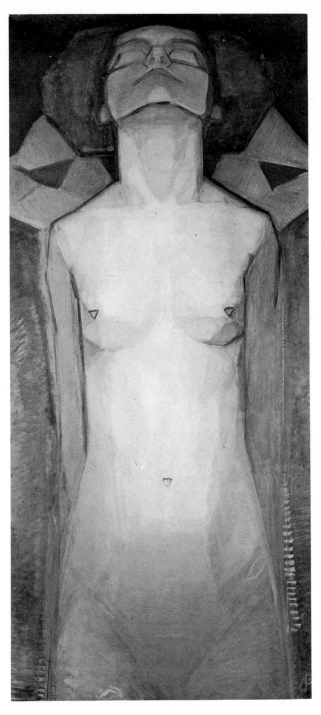

65. Piet Mondrian, *Evolution*, triptych, 1911.

66. Edvard Munch, *Woman (Sphinx)*, 1899.

67. Jan Toorop, *The Three Brides*, 1893.

66

67

68. Frank Kupka, *Vertical Planes in Blue and Red*, 1913.

69. Edward Gordon Craig, Stage design for *Hamlet*, project, 1908.

68

69

70. Piet Mondrian, *Lighthouse at Westkapelle*, 1908.

71. Frank Kupka, *Nocturne*, 1911.

72. Frank Kupka, *Keyboard Landscape*, 1909.

71

72

[125]

73. Frank Kupka, *Nocturne*, 1900.

74. Frank Kupka, *Amorpha, Fugue in Two Colors*, 1912.

75. Henry van de Velde, *Abstract Composition*, c. 1890.

74

75

[127]

76. Hans Schmithals, *Composition*, c. 1900.

ficially artistic and his embodiment of the gist of the work in a plain ('unartistic') reproduction of the straightforward solid object."[5] The new idealism—geometric abstraction—met its counterpart in a new realism.

And what, in the light of these principles, were the attitudes actually adopted by artists? Although the polarity postulated by Kandinsky was taken to its uttermost limits by Mondrian and Duchamp, the extremities of Grand Realism and Grand Abstraction were nevertheless far from absorbing all the available creative impetus.[6] A number of important artists, in other words, were prepared to compromise and to apply themselves to the terrain between these poles, experimenting—quite in accord with Kandinsky's elective freedom—with "many combinations of the differing consonances between abstraction and realism."[7] That amounted to an effort to bridge the gap only just opened between a picture's formal and factual contents and to prevent, in Kandinsky's language, the two "scales of the balance" from drifting apart. Yet painters who took this line did not try to maintain an equilibrium between the "purely artistic" and "objective" factors; preeminence was ceded to the former. In that way, formal contents were sufficiently prominent so that they did not merge with factual ones and could therefore be set off against them. In the act of perception the viewer was expected to disengage the formal from the factual contents and to relate afresh the distinctive value of the form to the object depicted. That constituted his contribution to elucidation of the picture.

The reintegration of form and object took place at diverse levels of expression whose idiom was to be traced back to Analytical Cubism. A number of Parisian painters made the start: Léger, Delaunay, Villon, Duchamp, Picabia, and Chagall.[8] They made up their minds to elaborate Cubism's formal, chromatic, and poetic rules of composition. Ferdinand Léger wanted to restore to pictorial elements their well-rounded, stereometric compactness

(*Ill. 110*) and earned for his pains the derisory epithet *tubiste* ("piping painter"). Robert Delaunay decided to attempt a rhythmically expressive transformation of the Cubist axes. He employed luminosity of color, neglected by Picasso and Braque, to intensify the ideal consonance that he perceived in the dynamism of modern life (*Ills. 111–112*). Jacques Villon drew on Cubism's prismatic forms for the creation of his fine-spun tissue of lines (*Ill. 113*) which was related to Lyonel Feininger's gothicized Cubism (*Ill. 114*). Villon's half-brother, Marcel Duchamp, and Picabia took for their starting point the hermetic aspects of Analytical Cubism and produced enigmatic, metamorphic hybrids (*Ills. 115–116*). Marc Chagall deduced from the Cubists' principle of simultaneousness, which allowed for coexistence of a number of views of the same object, a poetic simultaneity enabling him to present actual happenings, memories, and the stuff of dreams in a manner of Cubist interpenetration (*Ill. 117*).

In Italy and in Germany, too, Cubism underwent reassessment. The Futurists admired Picasso and Braque, but complained that "they insist on painting the motionless, the congealed, and all the static circumstances of nature." For themselves they claimed that "we on the other hand seek from points of view single-mindedly fraught with the future for a style of motion, a thing which has never been attempted before us."[9] For the realization of their creative purposes they employed "dynamic hieroglyphics" (*Ills. 57, 118*). The range of this vocabulary extended from flowing lines and billows of color to Cubist angles and sharply thrusting forms, with the difference that these now underwent hectic dramatization. In the Blaue Reiter circle, too, criticism was mingled with admiration for Cubist doctrine. "The creation of a new canon which shall bestow style and inner beauty on our lives"—Roger Allard's formulation of the French avant-garde's message to readers of the Blaue Reiter almanac[10]—was not regarded as the ultimate goal.

Regardless of his own commitment to Cubism, Franz Marc

prophesied an early doom for those who clung to Cubist and other programs. Marc wanted to thrust forward into more recondite reaches of significance and his ambition was "to furnish symbols appropriate to the altars of the coming religion of the intellect behind whose manifestation their technical creator disappears."[11] Therefore his admiration for a Cubist Picasso was not aroused by the picture's geometric computation, but its disclosure of the "mystically inner construction" in the conception of the world.

Some of Marc's own paintings imparted to the Cubist modes of expression an irrational trend toward romanticized cosmic realms of experience, sometimes resulting in contiguity with the dynamic lineation of the Futurists (*Ill. 52*). Others took their cosmic cue from older sources: *Battling Forms* (*Ill. 119*) was a continuation of Van Gogh's incandescent brushwork (*Ill. 9*). Guillaume Apollinaire's dictum, "Flame is the symbol of painting," may also have been a source of this picture's inspiration.[12]

The exaltation of "modern life," propounded by the Futurists and by Léger and Delaunay, was applauded in Russia. The Russians sought a synthesis of western European trends under the auspices of national self-consciousness. In 1913 the Rayonist Michael Larionov (*Ill. 120*) proclaimed in a manifesto:

We deny that individuality has any value in a work of art. . . . Hail beautiful Orient! . . . Hail nationalism! . . . Rayonism is a synthesis of Cubism, Futurism, and Orphism. . . . From here begins the true freeing of art. A life which proceeds only according to the laws of painting as an independent entity, painting with its own forms, colour and timbre.[13]

The first Cubists also recognized that the time for synthesis had arrived. Juan Gris contributed decisively to clarification of the ambiguous, indecisive situation in which Analytical Cubism threatened to become mired. From about 1913 onward he tried, together with Braque and Picasso, to find a bridge from pictorial geometry to the world of everyday experience. The result was

Synthetic Cubism. Without sacrificing the power of their individuality, the compositional devices which had acquired an independent existence were once more brought within the range of object matter. They thereby attained multiple values and fulfilled various functions. The "shift" from one of these to another was accomplished through, and sanctioned by, the perceptual act of the viewer. It was up to the latter to decide whether or not he wanted to establish a relationship between a particular lineal or color structure and objective contents. Gris's *Still Life with Guitar* (*Ill. 121*) clearly exemplifies this. The curves indicative of the instrument's body also have an articulatory planar function. The central, perpendicular sheet of music is part of an irregular pentagon, the upper portion of which has been arbitrarily described insofar as it does not adhere to any objective contour but accommodates itself to the guitar's slanting stance. The sheet of music is transmogrified into an intrusive form (the pentagon) for which there is no factual congruence although there are articulatory pictorial reasons.

In Synthetic Cubism the concrete became decipherable again. The course of the contours was less hectic and more continuous than in Analytical Cubism—curves were again allowed, the range of colors brightened, the corpuscular fragmentation yielded to a clearly arranged planar pattern. The result was a "flat yet highly colored architecture" (Gris) or color surface construction, within whose *cloisonné* different layers of reality adjoined or overlapped one another. For the viewer that facilitated detection of the "finished assimilation product" (Kahnweiler).

Where Analytical Cubism had employed a hieroglyphic code and presented itself as a hermetic labyrinth, Synthetic Cubism became explicit. The gain was twofold: both clarification and simplification of the formal arrangement and poetic enrichment of a picture's range of content. Kahnweiler says that Gris himself called this way of painting poetic:

He embellished his pictures with metaphors, with "rhyming,"

as indeed he called it, drawing the viewer's attention to analogies that he had never before observed. Does not the mouth of this jug resemble the pear lying next to it? The sheet of music the strings of the guitar? This ace of hearts that glass? Affinities fetter things.[14]

Such visual puns could already be perceived in the multiple values of Analytical Cubism. Their aim at that time seemed to be to break away from one another, whereas now the tendency was reversed. The printed (LE JOUR . . .) and the written (VIEUX MARC) letters in Picasso's collage are ambivalent. Therein lies their correlation (*Ill. 97*). VIEUX MARC is affined to the world of facts and cognate with the glued-on newspaper head, yet the letters, released from verbal association and their expediently practical significance as "phonetic symbols,"[15] partake in the structure of the abstract "proto-lines." The same holds true for the printed and fragmentary newspaper head. In one instance it denotes a thing, meaning a series of letters whose sequence calls to mind a verbal notion with an empirical content familiar to French-speakers; in another, it is a constituent element ranking on equal terms with the picture's abstract elements. In other words the letters L, E, J, O, U, and R function, as soon as their conventional meaning has been forgotten, as abstract or, more properly, autonomous pictorial ciphers. From this ambivalence Synthetic Cubism evolved the poetic symbiosis between the "purely artistic" and the "objective."

The desire for synthesis, integration, and consolidation of the newly won ground was not confined to artists. On a wide front "consumers," too, the broad-minded sections of the general public and world of critics, showed themselves receptive. Proof of that is furnished by a number of comprehensively planned exhibition events. In 1911 and 1912 the two Blaue Reiter shows took place at Munich [16]; in 1912 the Sonderbund exhibition at Cologne[17]; in 1913, inspired by the foregoing, the Armory Show at New York[18]; and, also in 1913, Herwarth Walden's Erster Deutsche Herbstsalon

[133]

(First German Autumn Salon) at Berlin.[19] These surveys, organized with much expert knowledge and magnanimity of spirit, revealed the conviction that a certain phase in modern art had come to a close and it was now time to present a balanced view and demonstrate the whole scope and variety of the new creative possibilities. The Blaue Reiter almanac was not content merely to manifest the international solidarity among the modernists. Seeking to anchor the present in the past, for the first time a global picture of the history of art evolved wherein the Fauves, Cubists, Expressionists, and practitioners of Abstract Art rubbed shoulders with El Greco and Baldung-Grien, Japanese woodcuts and Russian icons, peasant *Hinterglasbilder* (pictures on glass) and sculptures by "primitive races." By integration of the present with a universal concept of history which—with Worringer—placed the urge toward abstraction at the outset of every artistic development, the contemporary effort was certified as having accomplished a successful return to the fountainheads of art. It is but little wonder that this pinpointing led—as a rule[20]—to clamant protest against all classical, post-classical, and illusionist art epochs and all the more emphatically invoked in its own behalf the plea of pre-classical forms.[21]

Some artists, it may be noted, extended the patronage offered by the past to include classical and post-classical periods. Their development passed from archaic to mature stages of form. Picasso's and Kokoschka's works of barbarization were succeeded by a reversion to subsequent and, in Picasso's case, classicist traditional patterns. Thus Cubism around 1914–1915 displayed rococo elements, and for a short while Picasso employed an Ingres style of drawing. Concurrently, Kokoschka was coming to terms with Tintoretto's mannerism (*Ill. 41*). This was the time when the Futurists were demonstrating the first symptoms of their imminent return to the still-life monumentality of *italianità* (*Ill. 122*).

More important, however, than the eclectic conciliation of

[134]

the past was the modernists' desire, suggested by Reynolds, "to unlearn, . . . [to] see the truth of things" beyond all conventions and approved patterns. Marc and Kandinsky set more store by original, naive expression than the empty routine that the naturalist and academic schools of painting had to offer. The attitude of the Russian rebels united in the League of Youth (1909) was even more radical. They were fascinated by intimation of artless spontaneity. Larionov used wall-scribblings and children's drawings for his pictures. He and his friends proclaimed their antibourgeois protest in the streets by taking strolls in fancy dress, their faces painted with flowers, Rayonist signs, and letters. In Italy the Futurists extolled the child, the lunatic, and the savage and directed their revolt against museums, the tyranny of rules governing harmony and good taste, and the canon of beauty derived from antiquity.[22] Behind this attitude of seeking to startle the old fogies lay an outlook that wanted to make a clean sweep of things. Its outstanding protagonists—Mondrian, the puritan idealist, and Duchamp, the ironic realist—were not content with rejecting convention and the academic line. They called art itself into question. Standing back to back, their resolve to prevail over the "art of works of art"[23] released forces that coalesced during the middle of the First World War at two points in the neutral part of Europe. On February 1, 1916, Hugo Ball founded at Zurich the Cabaret Voltaire, germ of the Dada movement, and on June 16, 1917, the first number of the Dutch group's periodical, *De Stijl*, was published.

As well as their common point of departure—Cubism—the two paths diverging toward "lawful beauty" and "truth to life" had many intermediate goals in common. Dissatisfaction with the ornamental, unrealistic role of the ordinary work of art and the rejection of subjective exhibitionism was complemented by desire for a fresh, more comprehensively purposeful definition of creative action. The formal impulse toward this reorientation is clearly discernible. The delimitations of Grand Realism and Grand Ab-

[135]

straction served to radicalize the dialogue between formal and objective contents and burst apart the hitherto carefully hedged reality licensed by art, thereby rendering the dialogue accessible to other than artistic realities as well. Kandinsky, even though the most deeply aware of the implications of this process, was not alone in observing it. On April 11, 1912, the *Technical Manifesto of Futurist Sculpture* appeared, containing the following declaration by Umberto Boccioni:

> We affirm that even twenty different materials can compete in a single work to effect plastic emotion. Let us enumerate some: glass, wood, cardboard, iron, cement, horsehair, leather, cloth, mirrors, electric lights etc. etc.—We proclaim . . . that there can be no renovation if not through a SCULPTURE OF ENVIRON-MENT. . . .[24]

A little later Apollinaire, in *The Cubist Painters—Aesthetic Meditations*, proclaimed: "Anything can be used for painting: a pipe, a postage stamp, a scrap of oilcloth, beer froth, colored paper, newspaper"[25] (*Ill. 106*).

Was the opportunity proferred by multiplicity of materials to be seized and creative action, even at the price of dissolution of the individual work of art as such, to find a place in the context of life outside of art? Whereas the majority of their contemporaries returned to the traditional easel picture, Duchamp and Mondrian, pursuing opposite courses, resolved to press on to total expansion of artistic creativity. The urge to attain a comprehensive penetration of reality bore fruit in two concepts. The one, championed by Mondrian, De Stijl, the Russian Constructivists, and from 1919 onwards by the Weimar Bauhaus group, did not expose art to prostration by life, but on the contrary delivered up the totality of life, nature, and the objective world created by man to the coordinative discipline of molding through form. The other, supported by Duchamp and the Dadaists (and subsequently handed down to the Surrealists), set out, in the name of life's incommen-

[136]

surability, to destroy the facade of reasoning as well as the arrangement of the world into categories inculcated by it, and to turn the reality of facts completely upside down (*Ills. 124–125*). The first group's train of thought perceived in life an orderly process of purposive lawfulness; the other, an anomalous chaos, adhering to no plan and permitting every license, with possibilities that are inexhaustible. The former argued the case for all-embracing order, the latter that for all-embracing anarchy.

Mondrian and Duchamp came to their own terms with Cubism (*Ills. 64, 123*). More important than their quasi-Cubist paintings was how they further explored a phenomenon of perceptual psychology which had already proved of advantage to the Cubists. This was the concept that every form contains variants whose respective validity depends on its context. Kandinsky provided the classic description of this remarkable manifestation of multiple significance:

If the reader will take an altogether fresh look at any one of the letters in these lines, seeing it primarily as a thing and not as the customary symbol for a part of a word, he will then perceive in this letter, apart from the practical and functional abstract form devised by man always to signify a particular sound, yet another corporeal form which creates a specific external and internal impression entirely on its own, that is, independently of the abstract form just mentioned.[26]

The letter produces by turns an effect of "functional symbol," of form, and of "inner echo" of this form. We should not overlook a remarkable anticipation of Kandinsky's line of thought. In 1907 Alfred Kubin wrote his pre-Surrealist novel *Die andere Seite (The Other Side)*, which was published two years later. The fifth chapter of the second part is dedicated to the "clarification of judgment." There we read about a new kind of wondering: "Alienated from its context with other objects everything gained a new signification."[27]

The removal of a conventional symbol from its accustomed context robs it of its functional significance. Kandinsky illustrated this by way of a parenthetical dash put in a wrong, that is, unaccustomed and unwarranted, place. The observer (or reader) is faced by a riddle and supposes an oversight on the part of the typographer. So long as the dash remains within the context of the type face and is measured by this yardstick, its transposition seems ambivalent, for "its practical and functional effect has not been definitely eliminated."[28] Acceptance as an autonomous form value has to await transference to completely different surroundings. "Let us therefore transfer a similar sort of line to an environment which wholly manages to avoid the practical and functional effect. A canvas, say." Following this suggestion, it is possible to apprehend a work by Mondrian—like his drawing *Pier and Ocean* (*Ill. 60*)—as an articulation of dashes (alienated from their accustomed context) or plus and minus signs and apply to it Kandinsky's conclusion: "So if in a picture a line is freed from the aspiration of representing something and itself functions as a thing, its inner echo remains unweakened by any subsidiary roles and acquires its full inner vigour."[29] Raised to the status of a "thing," the line moves into the vicinity of the world of things, meaning real reality outside of art, while precisely this reality infiltrates those spheres which were once the line's preserve, meaning its elevation to a factor of formal configuration.

What is the explanation for this reciprocal transition? We have seen that a line is a phenomenon of human perception which can discharge several tasks that in turn assign to it various strata of reality. Putting it more simply, a distinction can be made between a nonfunctional and a practical and functional sphere. In the nonfunctional sphere, where the line "itself performs as a thing," it remains independent of any object or factual content, belonging wholly to itself and its "inner echo." This realm of self-representation should be differentiated from the other where it assumes the onus for signifying certain "things" (empirical facts), and thereby fulfills "a practical and functional purpose . . . like a chair, a well, a knife, a book. . . ."[30]

While Kandinsky pondered the merit of the line as such, a complementary discovery was made in Paris. It was perceived that objects of practical use, too, had ambivalence and that besides their functional reality they disposed of a nonfunctional one as well. The Cubists were the first to assist in the visualization of this phenomenon. Grasping at the reality outside of art, and dovetailing fragments of bottle labels, newspapers, and wallpaper into their collages and montages, they propounded a transmutation. Alongside the original utilitarian purpose—which gave the deductive observer a factual clue—a new claim was put forward on behalf of these everyday, trite clippings from reality: they should be understood as pure form values and integrated with the pictorial articulation.

The broader consequences flowing from this new attitude are evident. If the "line"—granted with the qualities of an "object"—can be removed from its conventional context and thus be freed from the functions imposed on it, then the same possibility may not only be claimed on behalf of a dash, a bottle label, and a newspaper heading, but must be extended to every functional product. That was what Kandinsky had in mind when he conceded that an artist might use the hardest of three-dimensional materials and it was on this same equivalence that the directive of Kurt Schwitters a few years later was based:

A baby carriage wheel, piece of wire netting, string, and cotton are factors enjoying the same prerogative as color. An artist's creative power is exercised through selection, distribution, and deformation of materials. The last of these can occur through their distribution over the surface of the picture and will find support in dismemberment, distortion, covering up, or overpainting. In the case of MERZ pictures the lid of a case, a playing card,

[139]

or newspaper cutting becomes a plane; a piece of string, a brush or pencil stroke, a line; a piece of netting, overpainting, or stuck-on greaseproof paper, a glaze; a piece of cotton, softness.[31]

Accordingly, both lines and articles of practical use possess two strata of reality, functional and nonfunctional. The transference of a line or a chair from the "practical and functional" sphere into the nonfunctional one is termed formalization. How does this process take place in artistic practice? The Cubists, Boccioni, Apollinaire, Kandinsky, and Schwitters favored two- or three-dimensional hybrid products consisting of fragmentary articles of practical use on the one hand and form idioms (lines and colors) on the other. "Real reality" (physical reality) is first cut into pieces, then patched together again. Fundamentally this process of formalization rests on the basis of Maurice Denis' famous definition already mentioned. Modifying the latter, it could be said of Schwitters' MERZ pictures that prior to being a baby carriage wheel, a piece of wire netting, or a cigarette, they constitute formal elements obeying certain figurative laws (*Ill. 124*). Apart from this purely formalistic interpretation, there are two others open to an observer. The fragments of former articles of practical use can be seen in an ambivalent light, as form elements ranking equally with lines and colors and as intimations of the factual contents from which they have been detached. Cubist collages and montages exemplify such ambivalence. Or, ignoring every kind of formal dimension and configurative intent, it is possible to concentrate deliberately on the other extreme, the layer of meaning relating to content and material. Then it will be a case of wanting to encounter not any sort of conformation, but a conglomeration, and of being confronted with no reduction to order but vivid extraction from a reality whose nature is disparate, chaotic, and arbitrary throughout. From this angle multiplicity of materials becomes a simile for unvarnished, heterogeneous "truth to life" and serves as the dialectical counterpole to "lawful beauty."

[140]

This antithesis requires amplification. So far it would appear as though on a metaphorical plane "truth to life" can find expression only by the stylistic means of fragmentation and arbitrary linkage and, correspondingly, unimpaired, material reality is the preserve of "lawful beauty." This conclusion is rebutted by the facts. They show that the polarity mentioned becomes still more obvious should the handling of the material waive any act of fragmentation. What does "handling" in this instance mean? Again, two approaches need to be distinguished.

Within the framework of "lawful beauty" the Dutch De Stijl group tried to achieve formalization without alienation of function. Gerrit Thomas Rietveld's famous chair (*Ill. 127*) exemplifies this bridge between practical function and a strict and sanctioned canon of forms, as well as vice versa. In contrast with the one-sided formalism of a Kasimir Malevich—"A chair, a bed, a table are not functional expedients, but the configuration of plastic sensations"[32] —the emphasis here was on seeking a synthesis between functional expediency and plastic sensibility.

The other approach leads to Duchamp's *Bottle Rack* (*Ill. 104*). Once again it turns out that the transplanting of an article from its functional realm does not merely trigger off the process of formalization—as in the case of Kandinsky's dash—although it may well be that an observer will content himself with interpreting Duchamp's work as a release mechanism for plastic sensations.[33] More crucial is that ready-mades have several dimensions of significance. The intrinsic one lies beyond satisfaction of an observer's esthetic cravings for form and, *pars pro toto*, reveals graphically the utterly enigmatic quality and ambiguity of the phenomenal world.

Objects like a urinal challengingly champion unvarnished "truth to life." More precisely, they do not disclose new strata of reality in the sense of European painting's empirically realistic tradition, but by means of the tritely conventional reality at hand allow the properties of the unfamiliar to come to the fore. Whereas the school of realistic representation of reality had striven for years to invoke a bond of familiarity between an observer and the world of objects, Duchamp's aim was to render this relationship doubtful and to lend the objective world a two-tiered depth. An object like a bottle rack has not one, but—in Kandinsky's sense—several "echoes." Duchamp, by eliminating the act of creation, derided the *œuvres* category and in addition vented his irony on the functional rationalism which accords recognition to any particular thing only in one particular location. Hence the object of practical use, dislodged from its task, becomes the embodiment of the enigmatic, the absurd, or the wonderful.

Thus each thing has multiple value. That holds true for the parenthetical dash and the bottle rack alike, since both are susceptible to the act of dislocation. It also means, however, that there are no eternally established, immovable object relationships and that every "thing"—a line as much as a chair—is assigned fresh meanings through its circumambiency, that is, the objects of its environment.

The opposite results on which Mondrian and Duchamp, at about the same time, trained their sights can be traced to the accessibility of the whole aggregation of reality. Mondrian availed himself of the possibility of transposition so as to let the panel picture again dissolve into its nexus with architecture. What he had in mind was a completely homogeneous "beauty of relationship" from which the moodiness, grotesqueness, and tragic element in nature and in subjective sensibility had been eliminated. Duchamp, however, predicated precisely by the irony of his treatment reality's capricious traits and in his ready-mades and assisted ready-mades constantly divulged new links of reality. By so doing, he deprived man's entire arsenal of objects of its rational basis, emphasized its ambiguity, and used this as an excuse to indulge in innumerable connotative capers. Mondrian, the idealist, wanted to express ideas of lawfulness and godlike attributes and to exhibit a universal equilibrium. Duchamp made no effort to conceal his receptiveness to the Dadaist variety of nihilism[34] and his ready-mades were laboratory specimens of a philosophy which questioned every pattern of thought and type of reality. His was a case for adapting a thought from Nietzsche's *Genealogy of Morals*—this total skeptic became engrossed with and burrowed himself deep down into reality "so that one day, emerging into the light again, he shall be able to bring home the *redemption* of this reality, its redemption from the curse that the hitherto ideal has laid upon it."[35]

Marc spoke of "symbols appropriate to the altars of the coming religion of the intellect behind whose manifestation their technical creator disappears." Such were the meditative pictures created by Mondrian. Not for him the quest for godship in the ecstasy of subjective sensibility. He wished to portray its legislative power in objective images of form. His mysticism caused him to doubt the purpose of a work of art as such and to search for the lost meaning behind an act of creation. His puritanism bade him to invest Cubism's antisensualist, abstract, and idealist elements—Kahnweiler's "proto-lines"—with absolute authority. Accordingly, Mondrian ventured, in his delineation of form as in spirit, to the farthest and most austere point of Grand Abstraction.

Mondrian's attitude draws attention to yet another concomitant in the history of ideas. Part of his support came from the contemporary widespread transcendental longing whose catchword was supplied by Kandinsky's book *Über das Geistige in der Kunst* (On the Spiritual in Art) (1911).[36] Kandinsky and Mondrian were, moreover, preoccupied with theosophic teachings at about the same time.

At about that time, Worringer's book *Formprobleme der Gotik (Form in Gothic)* was published. It was an attempt to determine the character of the "Nordic will to form." Worringer paraphrased the architectonic concept behind Gothic art as the

[143]

trend toward spiritualization and contrasted it with that toward sensualization in Greek architecture. The "spiritual art of construction," contrary to Classical tectonic organism, yielded (it was alleged) a skeleton, not an animate body.[37]

Desensualization, dematerialization—those were the slogans in whose name the avant-garde desired to reveal again the spiritual, freeing it from the veil of materialism. "Back to Gothic" has been the cry of this type of effort ever since the Romantic movement, and it is noteworthy that the various, but by no means uniform, ideals of the Gothic Revival are indicative of certain tenets held by Mondrian and the De Stijl group. Gothic art, to them, embodied a depth of expression that, as opposed to the sensualism of the "vital beauty" of Antiquity, was thought yoked to the transcendental; on the outskirts of Jugendstil the medieval ethos of craftsmanship had been admired by Ruskin and Morris as having made as yet no distinction between high and low art, coinciding with the De Stijl group's doctrinal point of departure; and, finally, the engineer-architects of the nineteenth century had regenerated Gothic principles of construction by banishing the mural mass and transforming a structure into the lineal framework of a steel skeleton. Although this dynamism of lineal construction can be as little directly traced in De Stijl architecture's emphasis on the right angle as in analogous pictures by Mondrian, it is certainly to be met in the painter's earlier drawings and paintings which may tentatively be termed "gothicized" (*Ill. 64*).[38] Referring to these works, Mondrian wrote on May 24, 1943, to James Johnson Sweeney that a work in which verticals predominate (*Ill. 128*) achieves "Gothic expression" as a result.

"Greek architecture is applied construction," said Worringer. "Gothic is construction as such."[39] Mondrian tried to square the circle by looking for construction *as such* which comprehends *applied* construction. On the one hand he wanted to efface the last vestige of applied construction to which the Cubists with their inserted islets of objective reality still clung, to draw the "logical

[144]

77. Wassily Kandinsky, *Couple Riding*, 1905–07.
78. Wassily Kandinsky, *St. George III*, 1911.

77

78

79. Paul Cézanne, *The Large Bathers*, 1898–1905.

80. André Derain, *Squatting Man*, 1907.

81. Henri Matisse, *Dance*, c. 1910.

80

81

82. Aristide Maillol, *Night*, c. 1902.

83. Constantin Brancusi, *The Kiss*, 1908.

[148]

84

85

84. Oskar Kokoschka, *Murder Is the Hope of Women*, 1908.

85. Oskar Kokoschka, *Self-Portrait*, c. 1908.

[149]

86

87

86. Emil Nolde, *Peasants*, 1908.

87. Michael Larionov, *Kourva Manja*, 1907.

[150]

88. Maurice Vlaminck, *Sur le Zinc* (At the Bar), 1900.

89. Paul Gauguin, *Personnages Comiques* (from *Le Sourire*), 1889.

90. Ernst Ludwig Kirchner, Part of a letter with drawings to Fritz Winter, May 3, 1929.

[151]

91. Wassily Kandinsky, *Watercolor* (first abstract watercolor), 1910.

92. Walter Crane, "The Oval and the Rectangular Method" (from *Line and Form*), 1900.

91

92

93. Georges Braque, *Countryside Near La Ciotat*, 1907.

94. Georges Braque, *Viaduct Near L'Estaque*, 1907.

93

94

95

96

95. Paul Cézanne, *Foliage*, 1895–1900.

96. Georges Braque, *Still Life with Violin and Bowl*, 1910.

97. Pablo Picasso, *Still Life with Collage*, 1912.

97

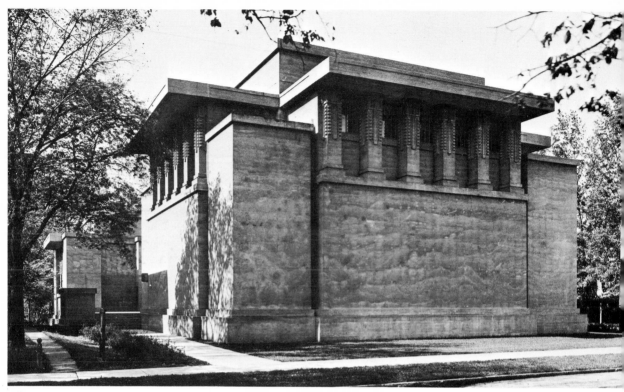

98

99

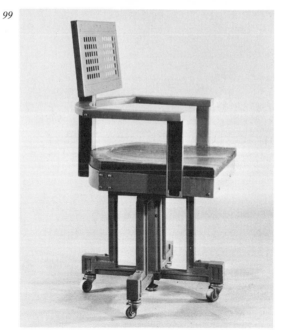

98. Frank Lloyd Wright, Unity Church, Oak Park, Illinois, 1906.

99. Frank Lloyd Wright, Office armchair, 1904.

100. Charles Rennie Mackintosh, Glasgow School of Art, library, interior, 1907–09.

101

102

[158]

101. Adolf Loos, Steiner House, garden front (back), Vienna, 1910.

102. Adolf Loos, Steiner House, street front, Vienna, 1910.

103. Adolf Loos, Steiner House, side, Vienna, 1910.

103

104. Marcel Duchamp, *Bottle Rack*, 1914 (reconstruction of 1964).

105. Marcel Duchamp, *Bicycle Wheel*, 1913.

106. Pablo Picasso, *Still Life*, 1914.

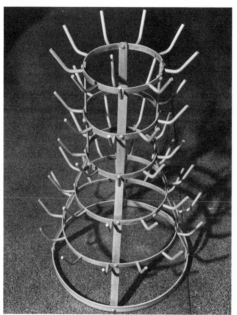

104

105

106

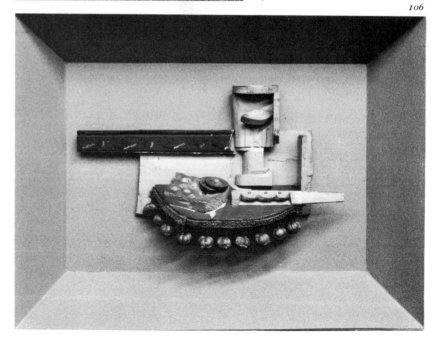

consequence" from Picasso's and Braque's discoveries, to purge abstraction, to lay bare and evolve it into the ineluctable expression of "pure reality." Yet, on the other hand, the panel picture, architecture, and the object of practical use were to evince a common form factor, showing that right-angled pictorial geometry potentially contained that element of "applied construction" on which, for example, Mondrian's *Perspective Géométrique (Ill. 129)* was based.

Mondrian was not content to express in his pictures that lawful beauty, in the sense of formal perfection, which is the delight of "disinterested pleasure." He seemed far more concerned to convey a spiritual message reaching beyond titillation of the senses and therefore equally beyond the representational conventions of painting—which engaged the sympathy of the spiritualist Mondrian as little as they did that of the "meta-ironist" Duchamp—the painting of "physical emphasis"[40] which luxuriates in individual sentiments and calligraphic charms.[41] For Mondrian a right angle did not have self-sufficient formal function, but provided a metaphor for his visionary synthesis of spirit and matter, man and woman, pointer to the law hidden from the surface of things and pointer to the Creator. "When one does not represent things, a place remains for the divine," runs a journal note of 1914.[42] This ideal concept derived from his uttermost consistency in adherence to the beauty of omission which Van de Velde defined as "negative" and whose beginnings are, among other things, to be sought in suppression of titillation of the senses and elimination of ornament.[43]

What Van de Velde had to say about "negative beauty" assists in comprehension of Mondrian. According to the former, a "maximum of symmetry and intellectual lucidity" will be attained by appreciation of the fact that the extrinsic negative form of an object—a piece of furniture, for instance—is just as important as the form of the object itself.[44] Mondrian's pictures lend this concept a transcendental quality. They evoke negative forms, forms

[161]

of omission. This renouncement of "forms" in the conventional sense (or in the Cubist manner of "applied construction") begets a void which the observer is meant to fill with that divinity which evades sensualization.

Mondrian set art next to religion as a means to "man's evolution." That was how he achieved the most profound and consistent realization of the new idealism which Apollinaire—without Mondrian in mind—in 1913 described in the following terms:

They [the young painters] discard more and more the old art of optical illusion and local proportion in order to express the grandeur of metaphysical forms. This is why contemporary art, even if it does not directly stem from specific religious beliefs, nonetheless possesses some of the characteristics of great, that is to say, religious art.[45]

Mondrian's resolution to preserve the "godlike" from profanation by sensuality was determined by his Calvinistic outlook.[46] This, moreover, prompted his contempt for a work of art's function of esthetic gratification and his distrust of the "natural," the world of senses and instincts. The urge to find metaphysical moorings for creative action, manifested in his proclamation of the equivalence of religion and art, went hand in hand with the search for fresh inner-worldly life and practical possibilities of action by the artist. This resulted in a twofold demand: reality should be etherealized and systematized while, simultaneously, creative performance should be emancipated from its merely ornamental, interpretative role and summoned to undertake the total shaping of reality. The *religio* of artistic creation desired by Mondrian was thoroughly Protestant in conception insofar as its criterion had its basis in the realm of the inner-worldly life. Applied art, according to his interpretation, was potentially a religious one and religious art merged in the total shaping of reality.

In July, 1914, his father's illness called Mondrian back to Holland from Paris, where he had been living for two years. In the following year the young painter Theo van Doesburg published an essay paying tribute to Mondrian's work. From this arose a friendly relationship to which Mondrian attached much importance. His "consistent extension of Cubism" had predestined him to be the intellectual and artistic inspiration of the De Stijl group. "So it was," Theo van Doesburg wrote in retrospect some years later, "that De Stijl, which hails Mondrian as the father of Neo-Plasticism, has become the credo of a non-national, non-individualistic, and, ultimately, collective power of expression."[47]

Apart from Mondrian and Van Doesburg, the founders of De Stijl included the painters Bart van der Leck and Vilmos Huszar, the sculptor Georges Vantongerloo, the poet Antonie Kok, and the architects J. J. P. Oud, Robert van't Hoff, and Jan Wils. Gino Severini joined in 1917, Rietveld in 1918. Mondrian and his friends hoped to establish a new compatibility between artists and the rest of the world, a new and homogeneously civilized way of living in which "plastic beauty" would reveal itself in "everything that there is." That was the tenor of the program described in an essay published anonymously by Van Doesburg.

Our magazine will thus bring about a closer contact between the artist and the public, as well as between the artists themselves, in the various fields of art. Once the artist speaks out, the prejudice that the modern artist follows preconceived ideas will be dispelled. On the contrary, it will be seen that the new work of art is not the product of a priori theories, but that its principles flow from art itself.

Thus we wish to pave the way for a deeper art culture, based on collective realization of the new plastic awareness. When the artists in the different branches of art recognize the principle of their basic equality and of a universal plastic language, they will no longer remain timorously attached to their individualism. They will go beyond this individualism and seek to serve the universal principle. And, in serving it, they will most naturally achieve an organic style. For the diffusion of beauty it is a spiritual rather than a social community that is needed. But a spiritual

[163]

community cannot be achieved without renouncing an individualism which is in quest of honors.

It is only by the logical and precise application of this principle, that plastic beauty can, through the new relations between the artist and the world, reveal itself as a style in everything that exists.[48]

The artist, having renounced pictorial illusion and spurned objective reality, now sought to regain the latter, though not as its imitator nor as its interpreter, but as its molder. What De Stijl wanted roughly corresponded to the challenge thrown down by Marx to the philosophers in the last of his *Theses on Feuerbach* —to interpret the world not merely variously, but to alter it. The expansionism of Mondrian's work, which remained preludial, may be clarified in something like the following terms. In order to attain the pure manner of expression of his meditative pictures, Mondrian had—in opposition to Cubism—freed lines and planes from their function as objective designations. He used lines, forming right angles, and primary colors as solely painterly means. That point being reached, he again integrated his abstract manner of expression with the reality outside of art and restored to it its practical and functional quality of "thing" which earlier, on the way to his meditative pictures, he had eliminated. Lines and planes were now equally to denote "things," tangible objects of practical use, and he showed them three-dimensionally as well as conveying intimation of universal "validities." The panel picture expanded—in theory, at any rate—into the wall configuration, the piece of furniture, and later—in the work of Van Doesburg, Oud, and Rietveld—architecture (*Ill. 130*). All of reality was subjugated to strict laws of morphology. The goal of the "new plasticity," after its victory over the "natural," was the end of art, meaning its self-dissolution. "And humanity will lose nothing by this."[49]

The issue was that of making a fresh start. As Mondrian wrote in 1919:

[164]

Even today some houses show a tendency toward Neo-Plasticism, but much time will have to pass for this tendency to spread to entire cities. Our surroundings will for a long time yet be deprived of abstract reality. Meanwhile, lacking something better, our salvation must be in abstract-realist painting.[50]

It was nevertheless intended simultaneously to act as a pointer for all other forms of realization. "Neo-Plasticism embodies in painting today what we shall later see around us in the shape of sculpture and architecture." How keenly Mondrian's "beauty of affinity" was opposed to the cult of the individual object can be seen from the following remark:

Formerly, the elements which articulated space were not merely means but things in themselves, objects with individual existences, and separate from the whole. These elements scarcely had any essential relation to the form and color of the room.[51]

Mondrian overlooked that he was simply enunciating a new phase in the consonance of form which, as regards the integration of reality, had already received Jugendstil backing. But, though Mondrian may have been at one with Jugendstil insofar as his concern for the total harmonization of reality, he rejected its belief in the omnipotence of artistic subjectivity. He was far more convinced of the provisional character of art.

Within the bounds of universal relationship a work of art was for Mondrian no more than an adjunct fit to intimate cosmic constitutionality. And when he said that "the abstract-realist picture will be allowed to disappear as soon as we shall be able to envisage its plastic beauty through the disposal of color in the room around us,"[52] he left no doubts about the redundancy of the individual work of art. We can recognize how this way of thinking, if taken literally, moves headlong toward a point of demarcation. The traditional concept of a work of art and its creator is being

[165]

abrogated. A new and dispassionate notion of beauty, linked to the functionally appropriate object of practical use and not the self-sufficient art object, is being postulated. "We see how pure beauty appears of itself in buildings constructed only in accordance with need and function, in apartment blocks, factories, shops, and so on. But add luxury and you begin to think of art, and pure beauty is destroyed."[53] If it is recalled that Van de Velde had extolled the beauty of objects of practical use and the "technical arts," coming to the conclusion that it was possible to attain beauty without art too, then it becomes evident that the De Stijl concept is a return to certain ascetic ideals of Jugendstil, or, rather, that in Jugendstil there was a propensity toward a breach of the esthetic sphere.[54] That is something with which the final chapter will deal comprehensively.

In Mondrian's vision of the future the ideal of form, called upon to achieve a flawless configuration of reality, turns into universal "realism." In a reality molded and harmonized throughout, that state is reached which Albert Camus, with inimitable pithiness, formulated in "Man in Revolt" as "beauty shall be experienced, no longer imagined."[55] The artist, by assuming this colossal role, at the same moment acquiesces in the limitation it imposes. For if art is the "manifestation of logic," as Mondrian wanted, then its function ends with its fulfillment. Consequently, in the future, materialization of the pure articulation of form will in the tangible reality of our environment replace the work of art. "Art is only a substitute as long as the beauty of life is deficient. It will disappear in proportion as life gains an equilibrium."[56] Creative man will no longer mold semblances of reality, but reality itself. He will no longer express the private feelings which prove him to be a genius and set him above his fellows. He will construct a new society, "a society composed of balanced relationships."[57]

The First World War was no doubt a potent factor in strengthening the desire for a democratic revitalization of art and society.

It also unmasked the hollowness of the esthetic and moral commonplaces in whose name the official representatives of Western civilization unleashed their strife. The sources of De Stijl's anti-esthetic attitude are nevertheless to be sought elsewhere. They are identical with those from which Jugendstil drew its ideals. And they derived from Britain.

William Morris, his mind full of an earthly paradise where liberty, equality, and fraternity should prevail, had thought it might prove necessary "to give up art altogether for a time." It was a condition which he regarded as preferable to having an art which as a status symbol satisfied the desire for gratification of a privileged minority.[58] Decades earlier John Ruskin, Morris' mentor, had done away with the notion of "art" by extension of its definition:

All that men do ingeniously is art, in one sense. In fact, we want a definition of the word "art" much more accurate than any in our minds at present. For, strictly speaking, there is no such thing as "fine" or "high" art. All *art* is a low and common thing, and what we indeed respect is not art at all, but *instinct* or *inspiration* expressed by the help of art.[59]

This reflection could have emanated just as well from Mondrian or Duchamp.

Just as "pure beauty," in order to become reality, can dispense with a "work of art" and manifest itself in the functional form of an object of practical use—as Van de Velde and Mondrian maintained—so instinct and inspiration can take the opposite path and not merely abandon "the help of art," but completely reject the formal creative act by putting a question mark over the world of existent facts by rendering it unfamiliar. That is what Duchamp did with his ready-mades. Affinities fetter things, Kahnweiler said of the poetic symbioses of Synthetic Cubism. Mondrian, Van Doesburg, and Rietveld wanted to objectify these affinities and accommodate the whole of reality within them. Starting with the

[167]

exclusive reality of a panel picture, they wanted to attune man's entire environment to a "figured bass" and thereby to effect an impenetrable "affinity of beauty" which would render a work of art superfluous. Duchamp agreed that affinities fetter things, but he did not toy with any ideas of an established and homogeneous system of coordinates. For correspondence of form, as when Gris lets a sheet of music coincide with the strings of a guitar, and a "figured bass," he substituted startling alienations and relationships between objects that common sense and the logic of practicality and function would relegate to the sphere of absurdity.

Duchamp, like Mondrian, sought escape from painting's self-sufficiency of function, materiality, and illusionism. ". . . the natural surface of things is beautiful, but the imitation of it is without life. Things give us everything, but the representation of things gives us nothing."[60] This note by Mondrian in his journal could equally well have come from Duchamp to whom the many-sidedness of things gave literally everything. Mondrian's comment is that of someone who sees painting as a means to an end, not an end in itself. For him it resulted in the creative act comprehending the whole of reality, but for Duchamp, in abandonment of the creative act. To convey his view of life, Duchamp, this "meta-ironist" (his own term), no longer needed "the help of art," but could be content with a playfully manipulated alienation of the objective world in order to put "facts without art" to debate.[61]

About 1912 Duchamp began to look for new techniques with which to impart his ideas, convinced that he would be able to express them more economically without the aid of painting. To the latter, relying on the use of material, eye, and mind, he denied the capacity to render intellectual affinities undisguised and without esthetic trappings.

His vision of reality nevertheless remained rooted in an artistic tradition. Doubts about the finality and monopoly of truth—in respect to our rational patterns of reality—can be expressed not only through the ready-made but also by artistic means. It is

[168]

merely necessary to recall the topsy-turvy reality relationships in caricature and so-called fantastic art.[62]

While Duchamp propounded his ready-mades, Giorgio de Chirico was in Paris painting his earliest *pittura metafisica* pictures. The enigmatic quality of the bottle rack was matched by these depictions of still life, streets, and places where familiar objects entered into peculiar and unfamiliar relationships exuding uncertainty and disquiet (*Ill. 126*). De Chirico cited Schopenhauer as his authority:

> To have original, extraordinary, and perhaps even immortal ideas, one has but to isolate oneself from the world for a few moments so completely that the most commonplace happenings appear to be new and unfamiliar and in this way reveal their true essence.[63]

And

> It is therefore possible to conclude that every object has two appearances: the current one which we nearly always see and that is seen by people in general; the other, a spectral or metaphysical appearance beheld only by some rare individuals in moments of clairvoyance and metaphysical abstraction. . . .[64]

This notion coincides with what Kandinsky said, with Grand Realism in mind, in regard to the material world's ambivalent character:

> If the reader will go on to look at whatever he likes on his table (even though it is only a cigar butt), he will be immediately struck by the same two effects. Wherever and whenever it may be (in the street, at church, in the sky, in water, in a stable or in a wood), everywhere the two effects will appear and everywhere the inner echo will depend on the external impression. The world echoes. It is a universe of organisms whose impact is mental. Thus lifeless matter is living spirit.[65]

Were these discoveries to be left simply to direct exposure through the pure "idea" (in Schopenhauer's sense) or to be brought into play in the production of works of art, that is, given esthetic garb? Duchamp tried restriction to the idea; De Chirico painted "metaphysical" panel pictures. Duchamp reasoned along the following lines: The ambiguity of a trivial object will be as much increased as it will be disguised through artistic treatment insofar as the formative process subjects it to an additional ambiguity. It will moreover be saddled with conceptions of taste. Kandinsky said, "Every form is ambiguous. The discovery of fresh and gratifying properties is constant and continuous."[66] Consequently discovery and interpretation of attributes of form will lead precisely to deflection from the basic problem, the idea. To which there must be added another factor: Inherent in the artist's decision to employ a particular manner of form, composition, and so on, is an irrevocable point of view, and thus a claim to interpretation, which forestalls the viewer and holds him in tutelage, that is, it imposes a particular attitude on him. For even though the work of art in question, depending on how the viewer construes it, admits of several explanations, it is in the eyes of its creator a definite statement. Duchamp rejects the work of art because he rejects the definite. His ready-mades are propositions about reality on recall. Through them Duchamp provides against everything that promises "solutions" and "answers." He contends, "There are no solutions because there is no problem."[67] There is therefore no progress, no evolution, no objective in whose direction the world may be altered. It is the exact opposite of Mondrian's hope for change in the world.

Duchamp accepts the absurdity of the phenomenal world from the angle of the "irony of indifference" whose points of orientation are the ready-mades. For Mondrian and the De Stijl group overall reality is potentially capable of configuration; for Duchamp every object is potentially a ready-made. But whereas Mondrian's effort at orientation seeks to cast a net of "beauty of

[170]

affinity" over every manifestation, Duchamp advocates a wealth of affinities that is rooted in nihilistic intellectual concepts. Since there can be no unequivocal, definite connection between things, the common factor between them is their uninterrupted, inexhaustible transferability. The correlation to this view is Duchamp's rejection of every generalization. That is why he refuses to recognize any preconceived hierarchy of values, any demarcation of categories, or card-index concepts.[68] His *Bottle Rack* not only puts a question mark over the sacrosanct sphere of works of art, but at the same time makes a conundrum of grouping objects of practical use. Every ready-made has its place in a no man's land outside of classification. Since the assisted ready-made allows for everything being reconciled, that is, coming to an understanding with everything else, nothing is basically compatible and there is no chance to become systematically and once for all master of the "complexities of reality," in Hegel's words. Seen in this light, the ready-mades attain paradigmatic significance. They are not simply a challenge to a game of interpretations; their isolation stands by proxy for that of mankind. That is where Duchamp's skepticism differs fundamentally from Mondrian's religious view of life and abstract generalizations. Duchamp's resignation sunders his aristocratic "irony of indifference" from the democratic dream of a harmonic "society of equipoised affinities."

When Duchamp arrived in New York in 1915, the reputation of his *Nude Descending a Staircase*, which two years earlier had been a notorious success in the Armory Show, preceded him. The painter, who had meanwhile been transformed into the inventor of the ready-mades, soon had opportunity to offend even his own New York friends. *Urinal*, which he signed "R. Mutt," was submitted in 1917 to the first "juryless" Exhibition of Independent Painters and failed to find favor with the Organization Committee; Duchamp promptly resigned from it. This was the period, between 1915 and 1917, when together with Francis Picabia and

[171]

Man Ray he formed a pre-Dadaist triumvirate which was as little acquainted with Zurich Dadaism as the latter was familiar with events across the ocean. The omission was not remedied until 1918 after Picabia's permanent return to Europe and adherence to the Zurich group, established since 1916. He came upon a group of revolutionary, restless spirits—mystics and nihilists, dreamers and reformers, wags and cynics. They included the poet Hugo Ball, the painter and poet Hans (Jean) Arp, the Rumanian poet Tristan Tzara, the painters Hans Richter and Marcel Janco, and the writer-doctor Richard Huelsenbeck, who transmitted the Dadaist spirit to Raoul Hausmann (*Ill. 125*).

The origin of the term "Dada" is a matter of dispute. It is certain, though, that the word first appeared in print on June 15, 1916. The German poet Huelsenbeck commented on the subject: "The word Dada was accidentally discovered by Ball and myself in a German-French dictionary when we were looking for a stage-name for Madame LeRoy, the singer in our cabaret. Dada is a French word for hobby-horse." The German philosopher Hugo Ball's version runs: "To Germans it is an indication of idiot naivety and of a preoccupation with procreation and the baby carriage."[69] These self-commentaries divulge the core of Dadaist philosophy. Since one and the same word in different languages assumes different meanings, thus representing a simultaneous blend of different layers of sense—it reminds us of the multiple value of the parenthetical dash and the bottle rack, and also of the caricaturist's technique[70]—every piece of reality gives the Dadaist an excuse to invent ever fresh layers of sense and nonsense.

Appropriate to conclusion of this pact with chance is that the group's view of life should seem foreshadowed in those circumstances which brought the Dadaists together. Adrift in neutral Switzerland, isolated from the warring European countries, their remote existence within the perimeter of belligerent preoccupation smacked of a certain alienation. The precariousness of this condition served to sharpen their eye for reality's dubiety.

The link between the Dadaists and Duchamp's dislocations was the revaluation of all values. The commonplace was to be made enigmatic, the conventional cast of taste—Leonardo's *Mona Lisa*, for instance—was to be rendered trite, and the ordinary extraordinary. As the finality of all established, stable categories of reality were being impugned, the sacrosanct precinct of the work of art did not escape question, the self-assuredness of traditional concepts of value was thrown in doubt, the esthetic confines of "beauty" were unmasked as the potential scene of platitudes, and the caprice of artistic creation was handed over for liquidation.

Even though the Dadaists were primarily concerned with enriching and fathoming life, they were unable to dispense with conventions of form in order to convey their intentions. Their "destruction of art by artistic means"[71] employed Cubist, Futurist, and Expressionist forms of expression. Especially evident are the borrowings from Futurism's anarchic dynamism, whose efforts to seize upon life's direct impact put it in a class of proto-Dadaism. The Italians originated the onomatopoeic poem, the exploding typeface, the clowningly satiric trait of cabaret numbers, contempt for set-piece art, and the use of multimateriality. Nor should the Futurist Luigi Russolo's musical cacophony (Bruitism) be overlooked.[72] The Cubists' contributions were the collage and montage techniques.

The urge to lay hands on the truth of life demanded doing away with all intermediaries and distrusted the work of art because the artist who wished to get at reality scented the danger of petrification and remoteness from life in every preconceived concept, in every creative plan, in every deliberation of intent.

By thus attuning art to everyday life and its special experiences, art itself is exposed to the same risks inherent in the same laws of the unforeseen and to its contingencies, the play of living forces. Art is no longer the "serious and momentous" stir of emotion, nor a sentimental tragedy, but simply the harvest of experience of life and the joy of living.[73] (Marcel Janco)

[173]

Arp's thesis was that it sufficed to obey the laws of chance in order to create a pure life.[74]

Hans Richter called Dadaism an "artistic anti-art movement." Were there, apart from the sources of form already mentioned, any other artistic affinities with the past which vindicate Richter's choice of adjective? For the Dadaists, too, the nineteenth century had paved the way. Their aim to achieve complete "truth to life" was founded on three affirmations of principle. First there was the doctrine adopted by naturalists and realists that every sort of reality was worthy of representation—"selecting nothing, rejecting nothing" (Ruskin). Second there was the antiformalistic tenet of Jules Laforgue (who, incidentally, had a great admirer in Marcel Duchamp), which demanded that art should mirror "even the confusion of life" and asserted that every keyboard of expression was legitimate (*"tous les claviers sont legitimes"*).[75] And third there was philosophical Symbolism, which surmised some deeper significance in everything that happens and an intimation of "zones of essence"[76] in every external event.

From a dialectical point of view there is yet another affinity with the past which requires emphasis and with which the ensuing chapter will deal. Dadaism can be termed a Jugendstil with inverse, that is, antiesthetic symptoms. Whereas the expansionist at the turn of the century, dreaming of the infinite overall work of art, wanted to imbue every particle of man-made surroundings with qualities of estheticism and formalism—his hope was coalescence of the work of art and the utensil—Dadaism equally aspired to the comprehension of overall reality, but the possession it tried to take clung firmly to the accidental incidence of the casual, banal, heterogeneous world of experience. As all of reality provided material for or could be the scene of Dadaist manifestations, art infiltrated life and life infiltrated art. The result on the one hand was "facts without art," on the other hand mixtures, linkages, and interpenetrations yielding idiomatic means belonging to a realm of expression that, borrowing a phrase of Bellori about Caravaggio, may be defined as "art without art."[77]

[174]

The Dadaists wanted to replace the conflict between art and nature with a fresh partnership. They aimed to create a continuum of reality which would veto the work of art's categoric, presumptuous claim to demarcation. Art was to be allied with the impenetrability of life and nature:

Dada is, like nature, without meaning. Dada is for nature and against art. Dada is, like nature, direct and seeks to allot each thing its appropriate place. Dada is, like nature, moral. Dada stands for unlimited meaning and limited means. For Dadaists life is the meaning of art.[78]

The quest for totality of life, while allowing the Dadaists to forgo conventional art, at the same time animated them to discover idioms expressive of the equivalence and interchangeability of art and life. New, untried means were not to be found in manuals of art history; life itself would appear to have fashioned them. That the Dadaists regarded as an important legitimation for their purposes. In the same way that any motion in life resists systematization, so in their eyes did creative action—basing itself on "instinct" and "inspiration"—possess authority for restless, uncurtailed improvisation. That led Dadaism, under radical and antiesthetic auspices, to realize afresh Jugendstil's ideal of lifting the barriers between categories of expression and endorsing their fusion. The avant-garde at the turn of the century was concerned with the dissolution of the self-sufficient work of art and its integration in an overall artistic achievement or else the flowing interpenetration of the practical implement, craftsmanship, painting, sculpture, and architecture. Dadaism, though at a different level of utterance, undertook the no less comprehensive effort of overstepping all bounds.

In the years that followed, our freedom from preconceived ideas about processes and techniques frequently led us beyond the frontiers of individual artistic categories. From painting to sculpture, from pictorial art to typography, collage, photography, photomontage, from abstract art to pictures painted on long paper scrolls, from scroll-pictures to the cinema, to the relief, to the *objet trouvé*, to the ready-made. As the boundaries between the arts became indistinct, painters turned to poetry and poets to painting. The destruction of the boundaries was reflected everywhere. The safety-valve was off. . . .[79]

Viewed like that, the conclusion can be drawn that the creative and experimental impulse of the Dadaist revolt, while directed toward questioning traditional "art," also laid bare the elementary and esthetically neither comprehensible nor definable "primal ground of art."[80]

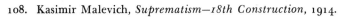

107. Piet Mondrian, *Composition in Blue, B*, 1917.

108. Kasimir Malevich, *Suprematism—18th Construction*, 1914.

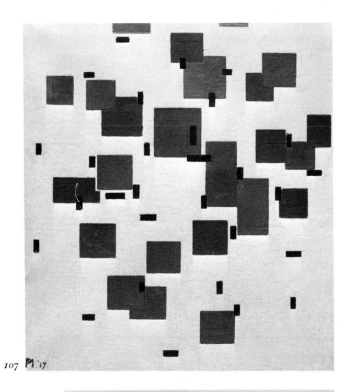

107

108

109. Richard Gerstl, *The Arnold Schoenberg Family*, 1908.

110. Fernand Léger, *Nudes in the Forest*, 1909/10.

111. Robert Delaunay, *Simultaneous Windows*, 1911.

110

111

[179]

112. Robert Delaunay, *The Team from Cardiff*, 1913.

113. Jacques Villon, *Soldiers on March*, 1913.

114. Lyonel Feininger, *Umpferstedt I*, 1914.

113

114

115. Marcel Duchamp, *The Bride*, 1912.

116. Francis Picabia, *I See Again in Memory My Dear Udnie*, 1913.

117. Marc Chagall, *Half-Past Three*, 1911.

115

116

117

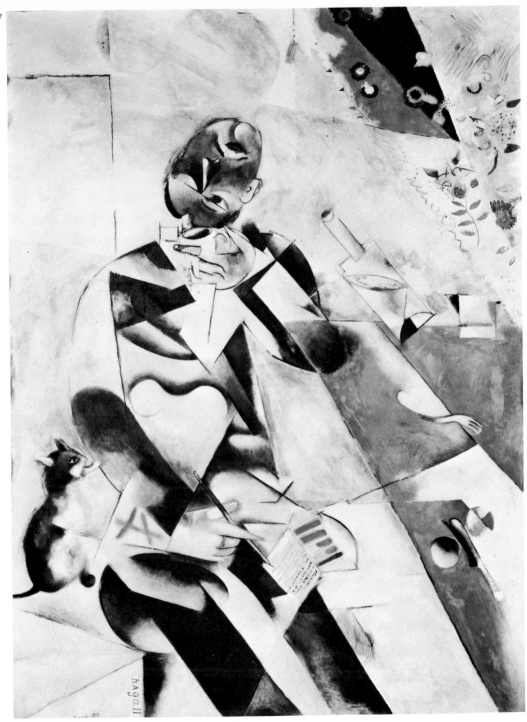

[183]

118

119

118. Umberto Boccioni, *States of Mind I, The Farewells*, 1911.

119. Franz Marc, *Battling Forms*, 1914.

120. Michael Larionov, *Blue Rayonism*, 1912.

121

122

121. Juan Gris, *Still Life with Guitar*, 1915.

122. Carlo Carrà, *The Daughters of Loth*, 1919.

123. Marcel Duchamp, *Sad Young Man in a Train*, 1910–11.

123

124. Kurt Schwitters, *Construction for Noble Ladies*, 1919.

125. Raoul Hausmann, *The Spirit of our Time (Mechanical Head)*, 1920.

126. Giorgio de Chirico, *The Philosopher's Conquest*, 1914.

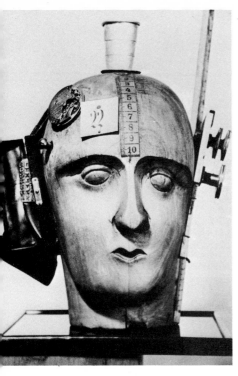

125

126

127. Gerrit Thomas Rietveld, Chair, 1917.

128. Piet Mondrian, Drawing in a letter to James Johnson Sweeney, May 24, 1943.

First aim: universal expression

Plastic exigence to this:
equivalence of vertical and
horizontal expression —
This is not in fig. A.
vertical predominates, gothic
expression result.

A

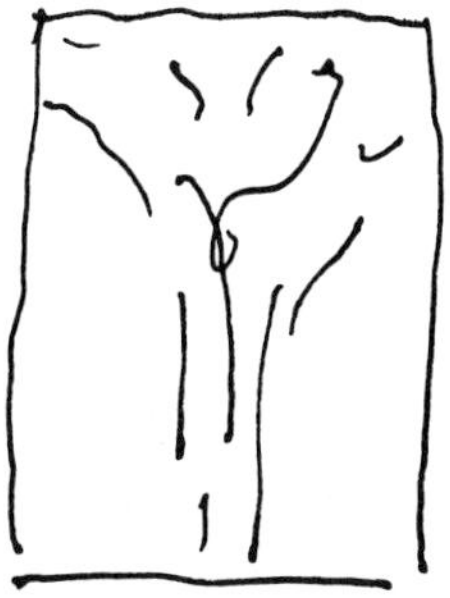

Second aim: concrete universal
                    expression.

In fig. B. there is equivalence of
horizontal and vertical expression,
but thus the whole is of more
universal expression than fig. A.
But this expression is vague,
for the vertical and horizontal is
confused. The structure is as lost.
In latest picture, the structure
and the means of expression are
concrete and in mutual equivalence.

129. Piet Mondrian, *Perspective Géométrique*, 1926.

130. J. J. P. Oud, House de Vonk, lower hall, Noordwijkerhout, 1917.

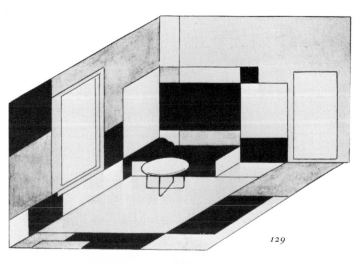

129

130

V

TOWARD THE ART
OF ARTLESSNESS

orms emerge from forms, and others arise or descend from these. All are related, interwoven, intermeshed, interconnected, interblended. They exosmose and endosmose. They sway and swirl and mix and drift interminably. They shape, they reform, they dissipate. They respond, correspond, attract, repel, coalesce, disappear, reappear, merge and emerge: slowly or swiftly, gently or with cataclysmic force—from chaos into chaos, from death into life, from life into death, from rest into motion, from motion into rest, from darkness into light, from light into darkness, from sorrow into joy, from joy into sorrow, from purity into foulness, from foulness into purity, from growth into decadence, from decadence into growth.[1]

Louis H. Sullivan, 1901

Le sens du mystère, c'est d'être tout le temps dans l'équivoque, dans les double, triple aspects, des soupçons d'aspect (images dans images), formes qui vont être ou qui le seront selon l'état d'esprit du regardeur. Toutes choses plus que suggestives, puisqu'elles apparaissent.[2]

Odilon Redon, 1902

The conspectus, which the reader was promised at the outset, now begins to take shape. In the first and second chapters it was said that the seed of the ideas from which the pioneers of twentieth-century art derived fresh inspiration, after undertaking

[195]

various radical "shifts of consonants," was contained in *fin de siècle* art. This is to contend that De Stijl stood in succession to Jugendstil's ascetically disciplined style whereas the Dadaists, jumbling together all categories of form, set out to revise Jugendstil under irrational, "chaotic" prognostications.

What was the nature of the influences that Jugendstil passed on to those artists who called themselves its vanquishers, and what was the frame of mind of the victors who participated in what they rejected? Anyone who quotes the ideals of a particular epoch runs the risk of hearing his own arguments called wishful thinking. In the present instance the aspersion can only be refuted by citation of facts, namely inherent structural features, which can be shown to have prevailed in *fin de siècle* art as they did in Cubism and Futurism and among the Zurich Dadaists and the circle around Mondrian and Van Doesburg. We have encountered these features more than once. They stand in a reciprocal relationship to one another, and consist of four concomitants: intermixture of degrees of reality, "disturbance" (alienation) of form, equivalence between positive and negative forms, and lastly, ambiguity in the means of configuration.

Illusionist painting seeks to give a homogeneously deceptive picture of the visible world. "Homogeneous" signifies here that the entire pictorial surface becomes part of the painting and that all the empiric facts are accommodated within a single, uniform layer of reality. Supernatural events, like visions or the performance of miracles, too, are represented as though the painter had witnessed them. Every element of form finds objective vindication through its manifestation in the physical world. But as soon as a painter abandons imitative rivalry with the external world, he loosens the close tie between objective content and form content, between the picture's theme and his means of conveyance, and the latter become invested with greater autonomy and self-confidence. However, before this aloofness from the perceptual world attains

[196]

its extreme in the abstract (free of objective meaning) picture—
once again a homogeneity of form—it passes through "many combinations of the various consonances between abstraction and
reality" (Kandinsky). Gauguin's *Jacob Wrestling with the Angel*
(*Ill. 8*) is one of the earliest examples of this process. What renders this picture significant is Gauguin's own testimony which reveals that the mixture of degrees of reality was *deliberate*.

With Gauguin, Toulouse-Lautrec (*Ill. 148*), Picasso (*Ill. 32*),
and Matisse (*Ills. 7, 21*), the mixture of various degrees of reality
was confined to the conventional technique of oil painting, that
is, the pictorial surface remained materially homogeneous. There
is a different approach which makes the pictorial surface materially heterogeneous and allows different kinds of substantiality to
coexist or merge with one another. In so doing, the painter need
not necessarily have an anti-illusionist purpose. Pierre Bonnard's
Dressing Gown (c. 1892) was painted on brown velvet. The elegant material is quite obvious for what it is and assists the painter's
effort at realistic reproduction, yet at the same time it serves as an
ideal surface resistant to corporeal molding. Even when the borders between pictorial plane and three-dimensional framework
become blurred, illusionist effects akin to the *trompe-l'oeil* can
result, as in the case of Julius von Hofmann's *Idyllic Landscape
with Bathers* and Max Klinger's *Judgment of Paris*.[3]

With Klimt, matters are different. In his easel pictures areas
of gold and silver, often modeled three-dimensionally with ornaments, adjoin zones done in oils; the Beethoven frieze (1902) and
the Palais Stoclet frieze (*Ill. 6*) have zones containing mosaic inlay,
majolica, metalwork, enameling, and semi-precious stones. The
critic Peter Selz has pointed out that this technique in some ways
anticipates modern collage and thereby the freedom of choice
allowed to a painter, as Kandinsky formulated it, to use *"every
material*, from the 'hardest' to the simply two-dimensional living
(abstract) one, as an element of form."[4] It is probably no mistake
to deduce Klimt's devotion to the use of luxurious materials as

deriving from his familiarity with applied art rather than Symbolist painting and sculpture. A French bookbinding of 1893 (*Ill. 131*) is sumptuous with mosaic, engraving, gilt, and enamel inlays—they are precisely the materials with which Klimt subsequently transformed pictorial planes. Further examples are seen in Mackintosh's work.

The following reflection makes apparent how closely multimateriality was in tune with Art Nouveau. An artist who turns his back on illusionism, retraces his steps toward an elementary form impulse which, though objectively undetermined as yet, has for its potential creative scope the whole of material reality; accordingly he will adopt at first one, then another method of materialization. But long before Kandinsky allowed the artist freedom of choice among every material, including the most inflexible, an article in the Jugendstil periodical *Pan* had singled out for praise among Symbolism's possibilities of expression that they enabled the achievement of "pictorial impressions" which, comparable with musical transitions, "do not confine themselves to a single material but contain the potentialities of all."[5] Any artist who follows the course of those concepts will not only reach ethereal regions of form—"reminiscent of the known, but not yet fashioned by the brain"—and from these proceed into abstraction's sphere, but will also encounter a far too little regarded possibility of mutual sense stimulation in the shape of those manifold enticements of multimateriality for which Kandinsky was to plead so emphatically.

The intermixture of different layers of reality is charged with a tension and confusion which the artist can conceal or emphasize at will. In a Cubist collage (*Ill. 97*), the arbitrarily inserted fragments of newspaper cuttings have the shock effect of foreign matter. When Klimt made use of "montage" technique, he had different aims in mind; in his case there was no abrupt collision between highly abstract and near-naturalistic pictorial zones because a common factor, the tenor of costliness and discrimination, stood be-

[198]

tween the picture's varying degrees of reality. That facilitated their unimpaired communion. As a result, Klimt's employment of multimateriality was neither noticed nor brought into relationship with Cubism's more radical application until a later date. It could be argued that at least one of the most exuberant inventors of Art Nouveau, Antonio Gaudí, anticipated the Cubist fragmentation of formal units. In several of his works he broke colored tiles for decoration into pieces, thus obtaining fragments with contours which were fashioned by chance. But instead of proceeding to shock confrontations between these arbitrary fragments and fully achieved forms, he reassembled them into new coherent wholes.[6]

To say that is to restate what has been already declared a hallmark of Jugendstil: the trend toward harmonization and palliation which seeks to establish an infinite concord stretching from cutlery to architectural layout.

Accordingly it might seem that the disordered form complex (*Ill. 97*), tingling with dissonances and interspersions, was an outcome of the supervention of Jugendstil and so a phenomenon accompanying the crossing of that boundary of form which helped twentieth century art discover its self-assurance. That is, however, only partially correct. It has been previously overlooked that Art Nouveau artists, whether consciously or unconsciously, often rebelled against their own proclaimed ideal of unimpaired harmony. Their method was to throw a particular line of form out of its course by exploiting the attractions of the unexpected. A few examples will corroborate the point. The Jugendstil artist, while professing the principle of balance and symmetry, made constant use of asymmetry to intimate that the form complexes of his creation did not signify any finalized, irreversible consummations. A dynamic, evolutionary attitude toward the phenomenon of "form" lay rooted in this basic concept: even if everything should stand in correlation to everything else, each individual form complex can represent no more than a stage of transition.

A fine example of the transitional aspect of Jugendstil is

offered by Josef Maria Olbrich. In 1899 he built a villa near Vienna which provided unusual devices for the display of paintings: "In the entablature, movable glass plates were installed at various spots. Behind these could be put any desired color print or other picture, which could be replaced to suit the whim or the occasion."[7] The facade of the Glasgow School of Art (*Ill. 137*) by Mackintosh furnishes a catalogue of such anomalous surprise motifs which invigorate the building and turn it into the scene of conflicts or attractive impromptu combinations of form.

Asymmetry and symmetry also coexist in the facade of Charles Harrison Townsend's Whitechapel Gallery (1897): the upper story's harmony is in contradiction to the round-arched portal which is out of alignment. A still more palpable example of "disordered form" occurs in Victor Horta's Maison du Peuple (*Ill. 138*).[8] There the staircase window of the top story is not symmetric to the central axis and in addition has been placed below the continuous horizontal line. It is disconcerting, rivets attention, and continues with all the remaining staircase windows, each of which has a different shape.

No less startling than the slipped window is the effect of a dressing table by Gaudí (*Ill. 132*). The dangerously poised mirror protests the axial symmetry of the table while the lower portion of the framework unexpectedly displays an interpolated profile. As a result the overall form of the mirror seems arbitrarily flawed in a way resembling the fragments of reality encountered in a collage. A sculptural theme by Hendrik Petrus Berlage (1903), laid alongside the stairs of the Amsterdam Stock Exchange (*Ill. 135*), takes an inordinately more complicated form—the outcome of the interpenetration of two hexagons. One of them (a), chiseled into the stone surface and with a diagonally symmetrical axis, is pierced vertically by an approximately hexagonal hollow space (b), distorted (that is, bent out of shape), and partially adapted to the hollow space's contours. The two hexagons together produce a complex form (c) similar to the interpenetration of objects in Gris's *Still Life with Guitar* (*Ill. 121*).

[200]

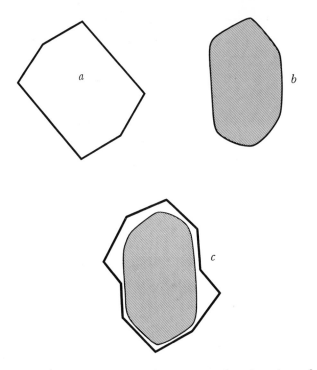

In the foregoing examples conventional rules of form are questioned and heterogeneity stands in flat contradiction to homogeneity. Symmetry is breached by asymmetry and thereby put in doubt. The slipped, "displaced" window and the diagonal, distorted mirror ruffle the viewer's expectations, introducing discontinuity and arbitrariness into a form complex otherwise marked by continuity. These disordered forms anticipate what Kandinsky said in his essay "Über die Formfrage" ("On the Question of Form")—a parenthetical dash released from its conventional function induces in an observer the feeling of "a typographical error, meaning something practical and functional which has been distorted." What purpose does such distortion serve? It is intended to help us see things in a new way, to disclose spheres of significance other than those of their conventional function, and to jolt reality and equip it with new coordinates of connotation.

A few years later Duchamp discerned in the ready-made the

possibility—via complete "distortion" (alienation) of the practical and functional character of objects—of giving multiple meaning to the entire world of facts. If the artists and architects of Jugendstil used the disturbed form to challenge the universal homogeneity of their creations, Duchamp maintained in a much more far-reaching sense that it was impossible either to codify reality or to reduce it to a single denominator. His ironic speculations on the multivalence of all mediums of human communication (forms, words, and so on) is reminiscent of Louis H. Sullivan's observations on the "fugacious nature of words": according to Sullivan, words have a peculiar tendency to transformation in meaning. "Statically words have little significance"; they need our responsive imagination.[9] Such a response is Beardsley's poster for Singer sewing machines (*Ill. 152*). The artist's pun on the name "Singer" is the subject of the design. In this work Beardsley clearly anticipates Duchamp.

The bottle rack's possibilities are not exhausted by its existence in a conventional, that is, practical, sphere; it is also capable of dislocation and alienation. The disordered forms of Jugendstil had already manifested a distrust of rationalism's and estheticism's view of life, and doubts about unequivocal, utterly predetermined form relationships. If this protest is seen in a broader context, it constitutes Romanticism's verdict on Classicism in the sense of Francis Bacon's aphorism, "There is no excellent beauty that hath not some strangeness in the proportion."

The equivalence of figure and ground is closely connected with the fourth concomitant, ambiguity in the means of configuration. This is demonstrable by looking at *Joie de Vivre* (*Ill. 7*). Two women stand in the left part of the central ground, one with her hand stretched toward the middle of the picture. An ascending line, continuing the gesture of the arm, begins just above the palm of the hand, turns leftward, and then, branching off, executes a rightward curve, accompanied in this maneuver by a suddenly emergent parallel. They unite and press upwards to the middle of the picture's border. What does this play of line convey to the viewer? At first he thinks he is looking at a tree trunk. But, instead of spreading into branches and boughs and bearing a crown of foliage, the line is transformed imperceptibly and without loss of consistency into the contour of a somber mass of leafiness whose trunk must be sought elsewhere.

The affinity to the world of facts preserved by a line of this sort is tenuous and revocable at any time. It can make its appearance at will and without warning, enter into partnership with objects, and yet dissolve the association very soon again, for it is its prerogative not to shed its transmutability. In the right half

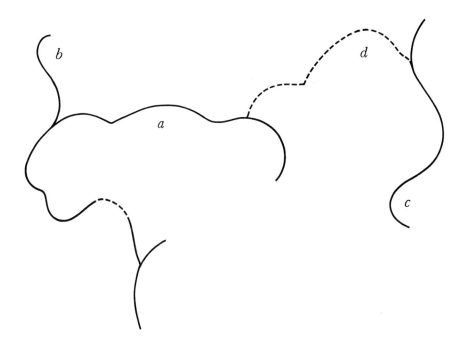

of the picture, for instance, one of the "contours thick as your thumb," which roused Signac's wrath, encloses a broadly spread crown of foliage (a). Out of this *cloisonné* a mounting tongue-shaped curve branches in two on the left (b), followed by a similar curve at the right edge of the picture (c). The sovereign arbitrariness of these lines affects the origination of planes whose nature is difficult to determine objectively. Sullivan's words are fitting, "All are related, interwoven, intermeshed, interconnected, interblended . . . ," and together with Redon it may be asserted that they signify "Forms which are appearing or which will appear according to the mental set of the viewer." Should the area (d) be conceived as intermediate space or as fully corporealized form? Questions of this sort dog the viewer at every turn in *Joie de Vivre*. Since the lines refuse to be pinned down, they only come to terms during the course of their migration across the canvas, now with the left, now with the right planar zones. More abstractly, the difference between positive and negative form, between object and background (or intermediate space) is neutralized and figure and ground attain equivalence, creating an "infinite rapport" which embraces the whole pictorial plane. This term was originally applied to a particular characteristic of ornamentation, the overlapping concatenation of form. It is not by chance, therefore, that the ambivalence of figure and ground should have been first identified in connection with Jugendstil ornamentation. In 1898 Karl Scheffler expressed the opinion that "the possibility . . . of doubling the pattern" results in "the area left free also exhibiting ornamental attributes."[10] Another theorist, Carl Matthies, wrote, in 1903, "What the true poet says between the lines, the contemporary designer of ornamentation places in his empty spaces."[11] These criteria, since the time of Gauguin and Seurat,[12] constitute part of the vocabulary of painters and graphic artists primarily concerned with endowing planes with rhythmic quality. And there is good reason for that. As soon as a painter no longer aspires to the illusion of spatial and corporeal effects, he must devote attention to the creation of harmony in surface. In a series of sketches by Emil Nolde, Goya etchings have been resolved into their planar values and light and dark surfaces produce an effect of equivalence.[13]

[204]

What Selz called "a most intriguing interrelationship of negative and positive shape"[14] is poetically matched by a passage in Nietzsche's "Sils-Maria":

> Here I sat waiting, waiting,—yet for naught,
> Beyond good and evil, stirred by light caught,
> Made happy now by shade, all but play. . . .

Artists have availed themselves of the opportunities provided by equivalence not only in practice, but have aired theories about it. Hodler's discourse on parallelism (1897) postulated the equivalence of form and interval; in 1901 Adolf Hoelzel published in the journal of the Viennese Secession his important essay "Über Formen and Massenverteilung im Bilde" (On Forms and the Distribution of Masses in Painting).[15] In the same year, incidentally, Riegl's *Die Spätrömische Kunstindustrie* appeared with its emphasis on the antinaturalistic trend to emancipate the ground and let pattern stand against pattern.[16]

In 1895 Christian von Ehrenfels issued the disquisition that was the basis for *Gestalt* psychology. This school of thought, parallel to the anti-illusionist turn in art and literature, sprang from rejection of the materialist theories upheld by the psychology of association and maintained the "phenomenal and functional primacy of the whole over and above all perceptive elements"[17]— a proposition identical with the esthetic theory about an artistic totality. Nevertheless it was only much later that *Gestalt* psychology heeded the problem of figure and ground[18] and research arrived at the recognition that thing and no-thing did not admit of any "permanent distinction" since "almost everything may at one time or another assume the thing-character"[19]—this, long after twentieth-century art had reached the same conclusion.

If equivalence of figure and ground were a matter confined to the easel picture and the graphic arts, it would amount to no more than a concomitant symptom of painting's regeneration on

[205]

"ornamentative" lines prophesied by Van de Velde in 1894. That is not the case. The "infinite rapport" does not simply rely for support on the *"arabesque pure"* (Denis); it spreads from the single object to the larger composite and from the isolation of a pictorial plane to the overall surface of wall-spacing, finally encroaching upon three-dimensional entities: "An individual piece of furniture will not convey an impression of unity unless all the so-to-speak foreign components, like screws, hinges, locks, catches, hooks, merge with it instead of remaining independent. . . ."[20] Nor does a three-dimensional entity conduct a self-contained existence. It communes with the other entities in the same space and—the decisive point—the materially intangible spatial area in which it finds itself, so that all of them coalesce with the "skeleton of the room" to become a "symphony," one in which (in contrast to "disordered form") there are no "unarticulated or false tones."[21] Further, the infinite rapport established in a particular space expands into the spatial flux, intruding from enclosed upon unenclosed space. The fifth of Frank Lloyd Wright's nine principles for modern architecture demands "a new structural integrity": "outside coming in; and the space within, to be lived in, going out. Space outside becomes a natural part of space *within* the building."[22]

Reluctance to accept the significance of these multilayered interpenetrations lasted a long time. The inclination was to interpret Jugendstil's "infinite rapport" as no more than superficial ornamentation lacking the vigor for spatial expansion,[23] regardless of Van de Velde's demonstration as long ago as 1898 that planar rapport was inevitably followed by spatial rapport.

An artistically perfect line as the border between two planes creates artistically consummate forms on either side. Take, for instance, in the contours of a piece of furniture the two lines that bound it to right and left and you have between these two bounds the piece's corporeality. Outside of them, on the other hand, you have a complementary form apiece, an incorporeal form, marked off against the wall and stretching away from the furniture to greater or lesser distance. A practised and sensitive eye will enjoy both, the corporeal and the incorporeal form, with the same degree of intensity and add them up to something that provides entirely fresh sensations.[24]

What Van de Velde, employing Art Nouveau's terminology, enunciated in these sentences was none other than the "affinity of beauty" which Mondrian subsequently deduced from Cubism's interpenetration of positive and negative forms. Like Mondrian, Van de Velde meant to reach out to the whole store of reality capable of configuration. He, too, without being aware of Ehrenfels and his school of thought, rested his case on *Gestalt* psychology's principle of the "phenomenal and functional primacy of the whole over and above all perceptive elements." Mondrian wrote:

> When we see things as particular and separate objects we wander off into the uncertain, and we are carried away in dreams and conjectures. One thing can only be known through something else. . . . So all we have to do is to consider each thing in itself as a duality—a multiplicity, a complex and, vice versa, each element of a complex as a part of a whole.[25]

The equivalence of corporeal and incorporeal forms is reflected most memorably and palpably in a direction of architecture whose incunabula include early houses by Wright (*Ill. 139*), the steel and glass constructions of the engineer-architects, and certain Jugendstil works. The historicizing eclecticism of the nineteenth century had concentrated all its attention on the embellishment of the plastic structure and had let the spatial conformation languish. The most extreme display of this shallowness is encountered in the chimerical facades of the Gothic and Classic revivals whose decorative complacency rejects the slightest correlation with the circumambient space. The unilateral emphasis on tangible values made intermediate space (i.e., Van de Velde's "incorporeal form") dependent on material form, thus space coming into its own at best as a by-product, unconnected with corporeal mass.

The engineering structures—Joseph Paxton's Crystal Palace (1851), Gustave Eiffel's Tower and the Halle des Machines by Ferdinand Dutert and V. Contamin (both 1889)—availed themselves of skeletal ways of construction and gave to space a new measure of self-assurance. The incorporeal forms—surrounding and intermediate space—claimed an equality of treatment. Space ceased to be something excluded and eliminated from the corporeal mass and became instead a potentiality of form with that mass at its service.[26] This shift of emphasis occurred parallel in time to the revaluation of incorporeal forms in the planar arts. The resultant equivalence of positive and negative forms was illustrated in exemplary fashion by Walter Gropius and Adolf Meyer in their model factory (1914; *Ill. 140*).[27]

The process developed in two directions. On the one hand it caused the involution of the negative (incorporeal) forms or rendered them autonomous. On the other hand the equivalence of mass and space had the effect of de-materializing corporeal forms in a positive way, somewhat parallel to the conversion of mass into energy. This process can be linked to philosophical beliefs which regard matter and spirit not as opposites but as interchangeable. "The world resounds. It is a cosmos of spiritually operative beings. Thus dead matter is living spirit," proclaimed Kandinsky. And Mondrian contended:

Since modern science has confirmed theosophic teaching that matter and force (mind) are *one*, there is no reason to separate them. If it is true that matter and mind (force) constitute life, we must take both into account, and not just one of these two.[28]

In this way Kandinsky and Mondrian spiritualized the instinct for form which had in Jugendstil already made itself felt as the champion of equivalence between corporeal and incorporeal forms.

[208]

131. Victor Prouvé and Camille Martin,
     Bookbinding, 1893.

132. Antonio Gaudí, Dressing table, 1885–89.

133. Koloman Moser, Desk and chair, 1904, Palais Stoclet, Brussels.

134. Tony and Pierre Selmersheim, Settee and book shelf, c. 1902.

133

134

[210]

135. Hendrik Petrus Berlage, Amsterdam Stock Exchange, stairway, detail, 1901.

136. Hector Guimard, Castel Henriette, Sèvres, 1903.

135

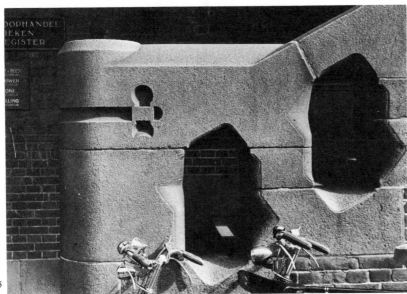

136

137. Charles Rennie Mackintosh, Glasgow School of Art, north elevation, 1896.

138. Victor Horta, Maison du Peuple (destroyed), facade, Brussels, 1897–99.

137

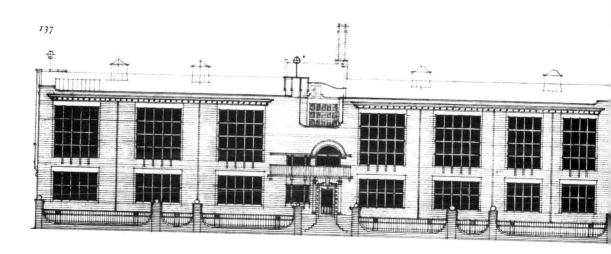

138

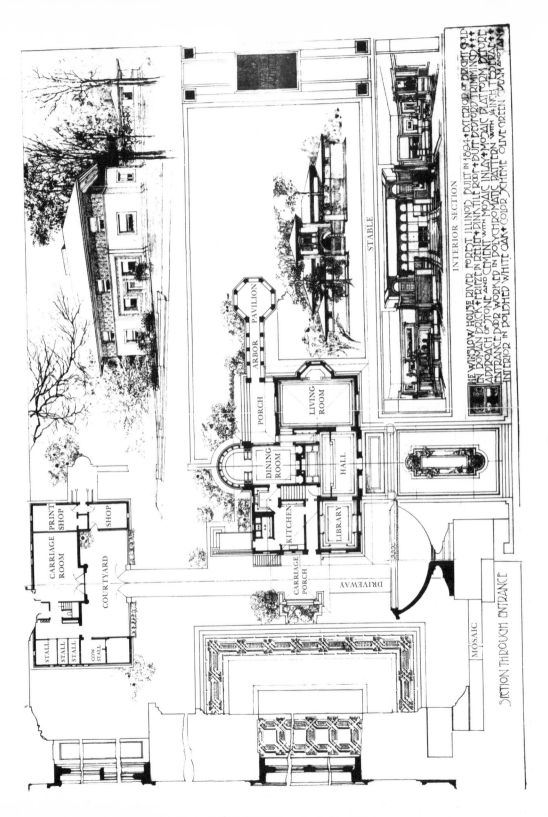

STALL

STALL

STALL

COW STALL

CARRIAGE ROOM

PRINT SHOP

SHOP

COURTYARD

STABLE

ARBOR

PAVILION

PORCH

DINING ROOM

LIVING ROOM

KITCHEN

HALL

LIBRARY

CARRIAGE PORCH

DRIVEWAY

INTERIOR SECTION

THE WINSLOW HOUSE RIVER FOREST, ILLINOIS BUILT IN 1894 + EXTERIOR OF BRIGHT GOLD IN ROMAN BRICK + FRIEZE IN RELIEF + DARK TILE ROOF + BUILT DEEP RED TRIMMING + APPROACH OF STONE AND CEMENT WITH MOSAIC INLAY + MOSAIC PLATFORM BEFORE ENTRANCE DOOR WORKED IN POLYCHROMATIC PATTERN WITH A RICH TOPAZ + INTERIOR IN POLISHED WHITE OAK + COLOR SCHEME OLIVE GREEN CREAM AND TAN

MOSAIC

SECTION THROUGH ENTRANCE

139. Frank Lloyd Wright, Winslow House, River Forest, Illinois, 1893.

140. Walter Gropius and Adolf Meyer, Model Factory, Werkbund Exhibition, Cologne, 1914.

141. Walter Gropius and Adolf Meyer, Fagus Works, Alfeld an der Leine, 1911–13.

140

141

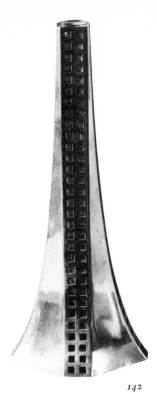

142

143

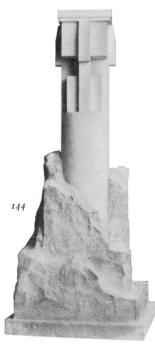

144

142. Josef Hoffmann, Vase, before 1906.

143. Charles Rennie Mackintosh, Willow Tea Room, Glasgow, 1904.

144. Hermann Obrist, *Pillar* (destroyed), 1898.

[215]

145. Paul Gauguin, *Still Life with Three Puppies*, 1888.

146. Émile Bernard, *Bathers*, 1889.

147. Paul Cézanne, *Still Life with Plaster Cast*, c. 1895.

148. Henri de Toulouse-Lautrec, *Parody on Sacred Wood of Puvis de Chavannes*, 1884.

148

147

149. Otto Wagner, Hofpavillon (Hietzing Station of the Vienna Underground), 1898.

150. Henry van de Velde, Title page from *Van Nu en Straks*, 1893.

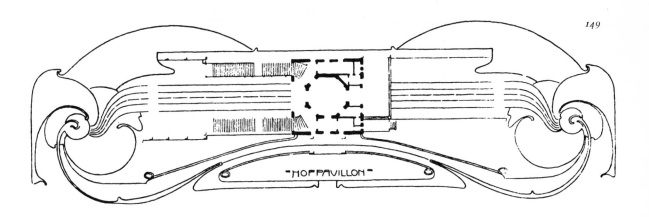

149

150

151. Arthur Heygate Mackmurdo, Title page for *Wren's City Churches*, 1883.

152. Aubrey Beardsley, *Singer*, c. 1898.

152

151

153. Paul Klee, *Two Fish, One Hook, One Worm*, 1901.

154. Henri Dumont, *Tous les Soirs aux Ambassadeurs (Yvette Guilbert)*, 1900.

155. Henry van de Velde, Belt buckle, c. 1898.

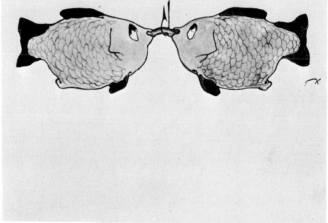

154

153

155

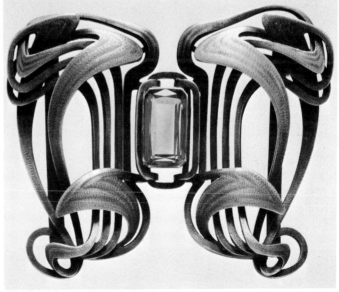

[221]

Sullivan and Redon described in visionary prose what Kandinsky a decade later epitomized in this aphorism: "Every form has many layers and the revelation of auspicious additional properties in each form is endless." These revelations too are connected with the repudiation of illusionism, whose didactic intent it is to render the most unequivocal report possible on the physical world. The artist's contempt for "naturalistic illusion" (Denis) demanded that a work of art differ from nature and present itself *vis-à-vis* empiric facts as an autonomous, self-reliant entity which obeys the laws of its own making. This was a view of the work of art that could not fail, concurrently with the autonomy of form and color, to hit upon its quality of multiple value. A painter who ignores, in his mode of expression, the descriptive factor in favor of an evocative manner of configuration reduces the unequivocal decipherability of his picture. Analysis of Matisse's *Joie de Vivre* leaves no doubts on that score—what the picture forfeits by way of fullness of detail and precision, it gains in autonomy of arrangement and evocative, poetic dimensions. When, in other words, the formal contents autonomously govern the objective contents, then the viewer, as Redon put it, finds himself "lost in ambiguity" and has to look for the "meaning of the mystery."

Such is the case with Gauguin's *Still Life with Three Puppies* (*Ill. 145*), in which "a flower on the tablecloth is repeated in the head of the dog,"[29] and Émile Bernard's *Bathers* (*Ill. 146*), dating from the following year:

Objects change their meaning in this picture: a root or garment becomes an erotic symbol. We observe in amazement that the lawn on which the nudes stand or recline suddenly becomes a wall for the figure in the upper margin of the painting.[30]

This "inversion" may also be observed in a work belonging to Paul Klee's Jugendstil beginnings, the watercolor *Two Fish, One Hook, One Worm* (*Ill. 153*).[31] If the stylized gills are seen as bridges of noses, the viewer is faced with two profiles struggling away from each other, their gaze not aligned on the hook of the rod but in the opposite direction.

In Cézanne's works ambiguity and "inversion" sometimes appear even to a higher degree, but they are articulated in a way that differs from Art Nouveau ambiguity. Take the famous *Still Life with Plaster Cast (Ill. 147)*. Whereas Liliane Brion-Guerry sees another plaster cast in the background of the painting, Meyer Schapiro correctly states that this is a picture on a canvas. Although Schapiro probes deeply into the intriguing ambiguities of the space-construction, he does not elucidate the spatial divagations of the blue drapery:

At its lower left corner, the canvas meets what seems to be the edge of the floor, but is also the edge of the beautifully formed blue drape and, by a startling artifice, coincides with the line separating the onion from its green stem (a stem fitted neatly into an angle of the drape). Through these devices, all frankly exposed, that whole region of the painting, which is built of straight lines, acquires an appearance of the constructed and "abstract," while other parts look more directly "seen." But these opposed attitudes do not clash, for the colors and forms of both parts harmonize and are inseparably joined; the most abstract regions have the same qualities of modulation and touch as the more natural parts. The blue drape, at once angular and curved, is also a liaison between the two.[32]

In other words: Cézanne's paintings can be more enigmatic and complex than Art Nouveau ambiguities.[33]

Architects were not behind in enlisting spectators' participation in "interpretative games." Otto Wagner's design for the Vienna city underground station near the Palace of Schönbrunn let the track unexpectedly run into a herbaceous ornament (*Ill. 149*). Still more disconcerting is the effect of the lineal multiple value with which Frank Lloyd Wright furnished the drawings, ground plans, and elevations of his early villas. The eye takes in a structure of indissoluble graphic affinity and gets its bearings via lines which continuously and unexpectedly vary the measure of their meaning (*Ill. 139*).

This capacity for transformation is not confined to two-dimensional design and cannot consequently be dismissed as simply an incursion of artistic embellishment into the geometric sobriety of draftsmanship. Kolo Moser's bureau cabinet has multiple value. By being so designed that the fauteuil is completely absorbed by the cabinet-wall, a spatial structure is transmuted into a planar element (*Ill. 133*). Hector Guimard let a window jamb of the Castel Henriette take an ambivalent course, straying imperceptibly from the window itself and becoming a spatially swaying curve that delimits the size of the oriel (*Ill. 136*). How simple functional forms discard their clarity and assume ambiguity can be gathered from Alfred Lichtwark's characteristically Jugendstil definition of a window: "A window belongs at one and the same time to the external and internal structure. It is the cardinal point on which the architect's design turns—or should turn."[34] This outlook expressed moreover the growing importance attached to "incorporeal form" when hollow space, not wall mass, was the building's "cardinal point."

No less replete with meaning, though normally more unsophisticated, was the expression of form encountered in Jugendstil posters and bookplates. Abstract ornaments transform themselves into human limbs without it being possible to determine exactly where the latter begin and the former end (*Ill. 154*). The most ingenious example of this transition in the two-dimensional field is probably Van de Velde's famous vignette for the periodical *Van Nu en Straks* (*Ill. 150*). No form is self-contained and each teems with transformation possibilities. As though he wanted to give a demonstration of this Jugendstil maxim, Van de Velde breached the right-angled framework and released the lobular, curving forms into the freedom of an open and boundless plane. Among other things the transcursion documented Jugendstil's rejection of the panel picture, representative of containment of

[224]

form. Here is another example of transiency, for whereas the majority of the forms appears devoid of objective content, echoes of natural phenomena and a loose roundelay of letters meet. Various connotations coexist. "According to the attitude of the viewer" some letters—the NU, for instance—can be deprived of their "practical and functional significance" (Kandinsky) while some abstract forms could just as well be interpreted as embryonic letters. Everything intermingles and nowhere can precise, unambiguous borders be discerned.

In the final analysis the discovery that forms and objects can assume more than one meaning leads to Kandinsky's experiment with the parenthetical dash, to the Cubist attempt to strip letters of their functional employment and to formalize them, to Mondrian's discernment that a thing can be recognized only through another (i.e., within certain contexts), and lastly to the paradigm of multiple meaning, the ready-made, and the "unlimited meaning" demanded by the Dadaists.

Further examples could be adduced without difficulty, and at the bottom of all these structural characteristics is found the view of life regarding the metamorphoses of form and spirit which Sullivan and Redon described almost coincidentally. Its support lies in the endless ramifications of a form impetus which is more elementary and at the same time more stratified than the limited, positivistic form alphabet at the disposal of painting and sculpture in the age of imitation of reality.

Where metamorphosis, interrelation, and interpenetration are the rule, there are neither hierarchic partitions between categories of expression nor explicit differentiation between art and non-art—even the borderlines between human achievement and nature's product, fashioned and found material, become blurred. Since nothing is self-contained and final, Jugendstil let the individual work of art merge in the infinite artistic totality. Inherent in the logic of this attitude is the loss of the prominence conceded

[225]

to the easel picture by the age of illusionism. The value of a picture as such was no longer the issue because it was now required to "fit into a room like a gem into a ring."[35] That was how, comprehending diverse spheres of reality and material, the most various manifestations of transitoriness between the second and third dimensions as well as between the various categories of art came to pass. A hatpin by Percy Stamp resembled a three-dimensional vignette, a door handle by Victor Horta a three-dimensional letter from a Jugendstil alphabet, a belt buckle by Van de Velde could, if enlarged, have served as a portal (*Ill. 155*). Arthur Mackmurdo used the flamelike lines of a chairback for a book jacket (*Ill. 151*). August Endell's facade for the Elvira Studio is reminiscent of a decorative tapestry and a vase by Hoffmann of a lighthouse or skyscraper (*Ill. 142*). Moser treated a bureau cabinet like a piece of architecture in miniature whereas Hoffmann provided the structural block of the Palais Stoclet with decorative fillets and bordered-on treatment appropriate to a costly piece of furniture. (*Ills. 1, 133*).

From this quality of transition the furniture complex or multipurpose furnishing developed; for example, a settee combined with a glass case and a book shelf (*Ill. 134*). Expansion of form enabled a piece of furniture to merge with a room's shell as did the interior design. In a music room by Richard Riemerschmid the table appears to grow out of the windowsill. Gaudí's interiors were pulsating plasma with various possibilities for coagulation and "protrusions." In his Glasgow School of Art Library, Mackintosh dissolved the wall into different lineal coordinates which erupted into the room (*Ill. 100*); in his Willow Tea Room the tables and chairs, comprised into framelike cages which derived from the lighting fixtures, constituted immovable functional islands or, more properly, comprehensive islands of space which were not only "autarchic" but also linked with the larger overall space (*Ill. 143*).

Half a century later prefabrication processes enabled the

furnishing aggregate to come into its own again. Designers will, for instance, deliver "the whole bathroom in one," regarding this as a segment of the universal "affinity of beauty." A passage in Wachsmann's *Wendepunkt im Bauen (The Turning Point of Building)* reads:

The large building fitted together from smallest components is a challenge to apply this principle to the interior fittings too, which means bringing the built-in features, objects, appliances, furnishings, articles of practical use down to the smallest things into a directly organic and harmonious relationship with the overall structure in accordance with the conditions of industrialization.[36]

Omit the reference to the "conditions of industrialization" and this sentence could date from the turn of the century.

Wachsmann has in mind a continuity of interlocking functional units. The Jugendstil artist invented two- or three-dimensional continuities of form where imagination was allowed to rise above practical demands. That introduced a fresh perspective. Kandinsky and Duchamp showed how it is possible to see an object freed from any practical purpose. That was something that, in principle, estheticism had anticipated, for as soon as the object of practical use aspired to the dignity of a work of art there supervened that concealment of function which Duchamp and Kandinsky wanted to evoke by alienating the practical product from its surroundings. In Jugendstil, though, the concealment of function was not the consequence of dislocation but of luxuriance of form. Writing utensils, a candlestick, or a dish became manifestations of an exuberance of form that never gave their practical purpose the chance to obtrude.

The wishful concept of multiple coherence of form has philosophic roots (we can examine them now, after analysis of the fact, without risk of being rebuked for deductive speculation) which exalt it into a cosmic vision of multiple animation. "The world echoes. It is a cosmos of spiritually operative beings." The whole of creation, viewed from the perspective of constant metamorphosis, becomes the scene of an inexhaustible impetus toward form. The work of art bears witness to that too and trods a fresh path to the processes of nature after renouncing nature's outward appearance. That is as true of Obrist's *Pillar* (*Ill. 144*) as it is of the glasses where Louis C. Tiffany sought to achieve the effects of mineral salts and erosion processes.[37]

Nevertheless, the possibilities for artistic transmutation and fusion, though they may be boundless, reflect but a small part of that great event in form which Sullivan described with such power of words (quoted at the beginning of Chapter IV). The borders between art and nature are not set. What Sullivan said about the genesis and passing of forms can be applied with equal force to the genesis of nature and the artist's productive act; it concerns the biological processes of form and the adventures of creative discovery of form and its mutations. Artists, in abandoning illusionism, turn their backs on the superficial appearances of nature, *natura naturata,* and encounter the primordial and elementary *natura naturans* at the sources of their search. In other words, the *life of forms* exemplified in the work of art coincides with the *forms of life*—quite in accord with Van de Velde's hope for a "genuine union between art and life" and to which subsequently, straining in different directions, the Futurists and the Dadaists, the Constructivists and the Surrealists subscribed.

Not every period has the good fortune to find its artistic aspirations seconded by the enunciations of a contemporary philosopher. This did however occur at the turn of the century when writings of Henri Bergson. His *Matière et Mémoire* (1896) con-
the artists of the day could see their efforts complemented in the
tains principles such as, *"All movement, in so far as it is the passage from one state of rest to another, is absolutely indivisible."*[38]
That is nothing else than a general formula for Art Nouveau's

capacity for incessant transformation which ushers from object to object, from external to internal space, from corporeal to incorporeal form. That is a state of flux which intervenes in the stability of things and lets them seem potentially mobile and metamorphic: "We are given a *moving continuity* in which everything changes and remains the same simultaneously."[39] Since every concretion contains earlier and later phases of development, there can be no categoric classification of the material world and consequently no segregated species. Everything is in a constant state of transition: *"Every division of matter into independent entities with absolutely determined contours is an artificial division."*[40] Interpenetration is produced by a coalescent force which Bergson traced to a single cause, *"vital movement."*[41] That is the theme of his great essay on *L'Evolution Créatrice* (1907). Bergson assumes the existence of an *élan vital* which is the source of all forms and organisms. This *élan* is at its purest and most immediate at the outset. The concept should be compared with the *"arabesque pure"* (Denis), the point of departure for the discovery of all artistic forms before being cast in objective mold and consequently undergoing constriction. And, together with Denis, it should be recalled that Conrad Fiedler tried to redefine the springs of the creative act and allowed the artist neither the right to imitate reality nor to idealize it, but simply to *produce* it.[42]

Bergson seems not merely to justify the biomorphic ideals of Art Nouveau, but to throw light on its material stratifications. At the beginning, he says, the "initial impulse of life is above all directed toward freedom of action."[43] Thus it accords with those elementary forms of which a Jugendstil spokesman proclaimed that "they are not confined to a single material, but contain the potentiality of all materials."[44] In its total disposability this *élan vital* corresponds to the freedom that Van de Velde claimed on behalf of the ornament, the freedom to represent nothing whatever. Sooner or later the *élan* meets with resistance from matter and is either hampered or deflected by it. Gradually consolidated into the matter thereby, it appears to split into species that think only of themselves but are secretly interlocked in an incessant "reciprocal interpenetration."[45] Kandinsky contended that the spirit disposed of an entire "store" and that, therefore, the artist could employ *"every material,* from the 'hardest' to the simply two-dimensional living (abstract) one, as an element of form." Bergson furnished his *élan vital* with a similar freedom of choice: "Its choice [of matter] will never be definitive: it will leap indefinitely from one to the other."[46]

VI

CONCLUSIONS

ur book began with a confrontation between Matisse and Klimt. As is the case with every comparison, there was a choice between two contrary points of view. One, seeking factors in common, disregarded separative aspects; the other unraveled divergencies between the two painters and the trends that they represented. The questions posed consequently produced complementary though incomplete answers. To compare Klimt and Matisse by actual example served nevertheless to set out the key problems which have recurrently engaged our attention. We shall now discuss the broader principles involved.

The preceding chapter showed how, with the aid of certain structural characteristics, it was possible to trace connections between Art Nouveau and Abstract Art, Constructivism, Dadaism, Duchamp, and Mondrian. Prerequisite to this comparison, though, consideration of that bridge in the evolution of form which runs between these connections was deliberately omitted.

This method of omission is justified when it serves to demonstrate the continuity of the problems of form and content in the period from about 1890 to 1917. At this stage it is however equally essential to provide a supplementary perspective. Precisely because continuity and stagnation are not identical, and therefore there are changes to record between 1890 and 1917, we must once more examine the "bridge of form," seeing its crossing as the event by which we think ourselves able to recognize the historical forces advancing into unknown territory. This "bridge of form" divides the twentieth century from its antecedents. Its effect is, to give just one instance, that pictures by Kandinsky (*Ill. 91*) and Mondrian (*Ill. 59*) stand in direct relationship to our contemporary world whereas the abstract works at the turn of the century (*Ill. 75*) appear to have halted in a historically sundered anteroom. How is this terrain, from which the pioneers of our century cast off in the decisive years between 1905 and 1911, to be demarcated?

Taking the criteria of conventional form analysis, based on or derived from panel painting, the outgoing nineteenth century presents the following picture: Certain painters, unknown or suspect to the world of their time, dissent from the comparatively homogeneous image displayed by an international climate of taste (Jugendstil, Art Nouveau). Their mode of expression is a revolt against pliant, precious, and often fatally feasible panestheticism. The gap between Van Gogh, Gauguin, Munch and Cézanne, and the urbane form idiom of a Tiffany, Riemerschmid, Gaudí, or Mackintosh is so obvious and the posthumous share of the former group of painters in the rise of Fauvism, Expressionism, and Cubism is subsequently (between 1905 and 1908) so great that it is a recurrent temptation to ascribe to these painters the sole credit for the laying of the foundations of twentieth-century art and to deny Jugendstil any part in this development.

Our analysis of pictures in the first chapter suffices to discount such an interpretation. Picasso's words, already quoted, apply to all the artists considered there and to all varieties of the revolt against the formulary character of Jugendstil:

We were all Modern-Style artists. There were so many wild, delirious curves in those subway entrances and in all other Modern-Style manifestations that I, even though I limited myself almost exclusively to straight lines, was participating in my fashion in the Modern-Style movement. Because even if you are against a movement, you're still part of it. The pro and the con are, after all, two aspects of the same movement.[1]

That does not merely mean that Picasso, Matisse, Kandinsky, or Mondrian experienced their beginnings in Art Nouveau, but that they incorporated important thematic ideas from it in their later works. In other words, even though their resistance to the noodle style, as Picasso called Art Nouveau, harried them into a crisis of expression and thrust them toward the Rubicon of form, on whose banks Van Gogh, Gauguin, and Cézanne had already tried harder, tauter, and coarser means of utterance, they nevertheless remained within the bounds of the more comprehensive ambiguity which links—regardless of all differences of form—a picture by Cézanne with a contemporary vase by Tiffany, a Gauguin with a vignette by Van de Velde, a piece of furniture by Gaudí with a facade by Horta. The Cubist who decided against the *style métro* and designated Cézanne as his alibi took a distinct step forward into unknown territory of form, yet at the same time put himself in the line of succession to those structural traits which had already characterized the outgoing nineteenth century.

Seen like that, the labels alternately attached to the turn of the century disclose a profound significance. It is indeed correct that these years were *fin de siècle*, the apotheosis of an age, and simultaneously the point of departure for an Art Nouveau, a new art, a Jugendstil, containing the seeds of the great historical change in this century. Lapse of time enables us to recognize this fact. Events like Cubism or Abstract Art, which in 1908 and 1910 had the impact of unprecedented innovations, can half a century later be discerned as phases in a process whose beginnings lie in the last decade of the nineteenth century. An aphorism of Duchamp fits the fact that pictures with the passage of time present a different message: "An abstract painting need in fifty years by no means look 'abstract' any longer."[2]

The criteria determining this process were discussed in the

[235]

preceding chapter. Where it leads and to what degree it represents a historic rift will now be briefly expounded here. It may be that reasoning which depends on the "intermixture of degrees of reality" and other not very spectacular touchstones, though not lacking force of conviction, invites the reproach of triviality. It cannot help but arouse the distrust of the orthodox art historian. Used as he is to regard the history of modern art principally as a monopoly of easel painting and with scrupulous tidiness dividing the latter into -isms, not investigating any sort of cross-associations with other categories of expression, the delineated affiliations Gauguin-Matisse-Kandinsky and Cézanne-Cubism-Mondrian will be enough for him. Consequently he will dismiss Duchamp's ready-mades, Dadaism, and De Stijl as peripheral manifestations or interludes and, since our structural characteristics overstep the demarcated sphere of the planar picture and seem to plead for dissolution of the work of art, deny these traits the slightest methodological value.

We take up our stance before the fundamental problem on whose account this book has been written. What happened between 1890 and 1917 released forces whose effects continue to be felt today. It was a turning point of which, in a phrase of Ernest Renan, it could be truly said, "The child will still grow, but he retains all his limbs."[3] In those years around 1900 there came to the fore basic lines of an evolution whose consequences have as yet been inadequately appreciated by art historians at large. I refer to the overthrow of the easel picture. Its formerly paramount status has been forfeited and today it encompasses no more than a small sector of the overall terrain of creative potentialities. This statement should not be misunderstood. It does not diagnose the end of painting, but the end of the preeminent status painting has claimed for itself since the Renaissance. The triumph of painting over sculpture dates from the time when the "discovery of the world and of man"[4] (Jacob Burckhardt) demanded of the

[236]

artist the reproduction of ephemeral reality and therefore that category of art was most highly prized which knew how to adopt the closest external resemblance to reality's contours. Leonardo had already enunciated the factor which in the succeeding centuries ensured painting's effectiveness with the multitude—its capacity to marshal things in space, to render visible the play of atmosphere and light on them, and to mirror what was closest and what was farthest, the tangible and intangible.[5]

If the easel picture was illusionism's favored instrument, this planned illusionism was simultaneously the prerequisite to the easel picture's demarcation from the artistic totality. The positive result of this isolation was the evolution in form and content of painting between the fourteenth and nineteenth centuries. This leads in turn to the conclusion that the easel picture's position at the peak of the hierarchy of artistic categories must be forfeited again as soon as the illusionist dogma loses its absolute validity. That is what occurred in the final decades of the nineteenth century. Released from competition with empiric facts, the artist discerned that there are impulsions of form which cannot be established by objective analogy. Together with illusionism he dropped its correlations, man's central position and spatial perspective, and thrust forward into the realm of those elementary, pre-objective forms of which we have heard that they "do not restrict themselves to one material, but contain the potentialities of all." Neither guided by nor in tutelage to the nonartistic authorities of the world of appearances, a new measure of freedom took hold of artistic consciousness. No longer thinking in compartmentalized categories, it left the *élan initial* of form to undertake the most various material metamorphoses. Such an impulse can become tangible in stone or in glass, in panel picture or in glaze, and transform painting into sculpture, allowing the latter to pass into architecture. In short, the entire "material store" (Kandinsky) is at its disposal. Bergson's aphorism holds good for this *élan*, potentially infinitely changeable: "its choice will never

[237]

be definitive: it will leap indefinitely from one to the other." The beginnings of this historical process are to be encountered in the nineties; its deployment on a broad front was brought about by the revolutionary movements of the First World War—Dadaism in Switzerland, De Stijl in Holland, Constructivism in Russia. It has lost none of its expansive strength since, as the multiple materiality in circulation under the labels of Pop, Op, or A-B-C Art evinces.

Whether the process signifies gain or loss depends on the point of view of the beholder. Those who adhere to the illusionist tradition in Western painting, which began with Giotto, accept in its train the categoric division between the free and applied arts and put up with the discrimination exercised against the second of these as well as the conceptual isolation of architecture, sculpture, and painting. Their outlook will lead them to regret the loss of prestige sustained by the easel picture and to feel bereavement at its diminished dignity. If, on the other hand, the artist is conceded a sphere of activity outside of illusionism which, on the basis of equality of rights, will lure him toward an interpenetration of architecture, sculpture, and painting, then this flexibility of form will be accounted a gain. This is the broad basis on which our contemporary world rests.

Assuming a positive attitude, the close of the competition with empiric facts means that the picture wins in autonomous purport and power. Maurice Denis' famous words gave this the force of an annunciation. The less a picture is a seeming reality, hence a second degree reality, the more is it an independent, autarchic object. The accent shifts from imitation to discovery of reality. During the course of this transference of accent there appear the four elements which anti-illusionism has, since the turn of the century, employed as its mode of expression: intermixture of degrees of reality, disturbance (alienation) of form, equivalence between postive and negative forms, and ambiguity in the means of configuration.

These four overlapping characteristics are symptoms concomitant to the interpenetration of categories. To regard this process solely from the angle of, say, the artistic totality, Constructivism, or Dadaism's total disarray, is to take too narrow a view. The key to the inexhaustible scope of interpenetration lies in Kandinsky's theory of equivalence and interchangeability between line and chair, i.e., between abstract cipher and hardest of materials.

Considered in that light, the decisive artistic event of our century has not been the frequently cited occurrence of "Abstract Art." Rather, abstraction has been merely a by-product of a much more comprehensive and far-reaching reorientation, the effort to abolish the barriers and differences of degree between artistic categories and to pave the way for an elemental quality of transition in the occurrence of form which will no longer give recognition to architecture, sculpture, and painting as distinct species, but simply as various sorts of consolidation in a single *"univers des formes"* (Henri Focillon).

To lay bare the roots of the most important thrusts in this direction has been the theme of this book. Analysis has been confined to a brief period so as to bring the historic change of scene into as sharp a focus as possible, yet without sacrificing its stratification to simplification. That has meant marking out the ground over which the last fifty years have traversed. Not that there has been an absence of fresh discoveries. There have been the Bauhaus, Surrealism, the fluorescent sculptures and paintings, the "mobile" architecture of the Russian Constructivists, as well as the wide field of kinetic potentialities. Nonetheless all of these ramifications can be traced to the premises which were worked out between 1890 and 1917. To have dealt with them down to the present day would have exceeded the limits of this study.

What historic significance attaches to the mutation for which we now possess illustrative material stretching over more than two generations? All the indications are that the absolute power of empiric illusionism and its varieties has had its day. Speaking

[239]

merely of imitation of the perceptual world, new regions of interpretation are becoming accessible to art. The same urgency of purpose as it applies to its own delineation impels it ever again to self-interrogation and to question its distinctive existence. A new era seems in the making which precipitates a breach with the traditions and conventions that have dominated artistic progress since Gothic and Renaissance times, north and south of the Alps respectively, imposed on the artist's priority on behalf of the perceptual world. The change of which we are witnesses, by providing a fresh and varied field of activity for those forces which for centuries stood in the service of imitative endeavor, looks back to that epoch *preceding* the outlook enthroned by "modern times" in the name of discovery of the world and of man; that of which the arts were then deprived is being restored to them today. Or, what was rendered accessible to them by this discovery has today to be surrendered again. In point of fact comparison between "modern art" and that of the Middle Ages reveals a wealth of characteristics in common—such as the multiple value of form, content, and material,[6] the blurred demarcation between individual categories, and so on—yet also displays profound differences. The capacity for the artistic totality is probably hardly any more extant nowadays. If medieval anti-illusionism had its justification in a relatively harmonious structure of faith, that of our contemporary world stands under secularized auspices and is lent support by individuals who imagine that their subjective views entitle them to take any decision whatsoever. That, however, is not the point of this comparison. It is the discernment that the period between 1890 and 1917 signifies more than the change from one style to another. It belongs to the great turning points in the history of art and as such it is on a plane with the events which gave rise to the transition from the Middle Ages to modern times.

NOTES

FOREWORD

1. Clement Greenberg, *Art and Culture—Critical Essays* (Boston, 1961), pp. 154–157.

   "The easel picture, the movable picture hung on a wall, is a unique product of the West, with no real counterpart elsewhere. Its form is determined by its social function, which is precisely to hang on a wall. To appreciate the uniqueness of the easel picture, we have only to compare its modes of unity with those of the Persian miniatures or the Chinese hanging painting, neither of which matches it in independence of the requirements of decoration. The easel picture subordinates decorative to dramatic effect. It cuts the illusion of a box-like cavity into the wall behind it, and within this, as a unity, it organizes three-dimensional semblances. To the extent that the artist flattens out the cavity for the sake of decorative patterning and organizes its content in terms of flatness and frontality, the essence of the easel picture— which is not the same thing as its quality—is on the way to being compromised."

2. Albert Aurier, "Le Symbolisme en Peinture" (1891), in *Oeuvres Posthumes* (Paris, 1893), p. 216.

3. Eugène Delacroix, "Raphael," in *Delacroix, sa Vie et ses Oeuvres* (Paris, 1865) (originally published in *Revue de Paris,* Vol. 2, 1830).

[243]

4. "By the late nineties 'Art Nouveau' had achieved a remarkable international success as *the* style of fashion and the avant garde. In the various countries it went by different names and was, in fact, ambivalently considered a national style or else an import from a foreign country, depending on a positive or negative attitude toward the mode. Only fairly recently has it been generally recognized as an international movement. In England . . . [they] called it 'Art Nouveau.' In France . . . it was referred to occasionally as 'Modern Style' and went under a great many names at first, such as the graphic 'Style nouille,' . . . 'Style de Bouche de Métro.' In Germany . . . it was the term 'Jugendstil,' from the Munich magazine *Jugend*, which entered the vocabulary. The Austrians referred to it as 'Secessionstil' . . . the Scots . . . named their corollary 'The Glasgow School.' The term 'Art Nouveau,' which was finally accepted in most countries, derives from S. Bing's shop, Maison de l'Art Nouveau . . . in Paris." (Peter Selz and Mildred Constantine, eds., *Art Nouveau: Art and Design at the Turn of the Century* [New York, 1959], pp. 10–11.)

I: FINALE OR PRELUDE?

1. Eduard F. Sekler, "The Stoclet House by Josef Hoffmann," in Douglas Fraser, ed., *Essays in the History of Architecture Presented to Rudolf Wittkower* (New York, 1967), II, 235–236.
2. Marcell Nicolle, quoted in Alfred H. Barr, Jr., *Matisse: His Art and His Public* (New York, 1951), p. 55.
3. *Ibid.*
4. *Ibid.*, p. 90.
5. *Cf.* two studies by Julius von Schlosser: " 'Stilgeschichte' und 'Sprachgeschichte' der bildenden Kunst," *Sitzungsber. d. Bayr. Akademie d. Wissenschaften*, I, 1935, and *Magistra Latinitas und Magistra Barbaritas* (Munich, 1937).
6. Henri Matisse, *Farbe und Gleichnis—Gesammelte Schriften* (Zurich, 1955), pp. 43, 48. (Original French published in *L'Intransigeant* [January 14, 1929] and *Minotaure* [October 15, 1936].)
7. Félix Fénéon, *Au-delà de l'Impressionnisme* (Paris, 1966), p. 109.
8. Edouard Dujardin, *La Revue indépendante* (March, 1888), p. 489;

Sven Løvgren, *The Genius of Modernism* (Stockholm, 1959), p. 107.

9. Albert Aurier, "Le Symbolisme en Peinture" (1891), in *Oeuvres Posthumes* (Paris, 1893), p. 215.

10. Walter Crane, *Transactions of the Art Congress* (Edinburgh, 1889), pp. 202–220, as quoted by Peter Selz and Mildred Constantine, eds., *Art Nouveau: Art and Design at the Turn of the Century* (New York, 1959), p. 10.

11. On the origin of the terms Art Nouveau and Jugendstil see Robert Schmutzler, *Art Nouveau* (New York, 1962), p. 8; Fritz Schmalenbach, *Jugendstil—Ein Beitrag zu Theorie und Geschichte der Flächenkunst* (Würzburg, 1935), p. 12.

12. Selz and Constantine, *op. cit.*

13. *Gauguin* (Paris, Orangerie des Tuilleries, 1949), Nos. 80–89. For Gauguin's sculptural and ceramic works, see John Rewald, *Post-Impressionism—From Van Gogh to Gauguin* (New York, 1956), p. 441 and Bibliography, p. 567.

II: THE PIONEERS AND THEIR NINETEENTH-CENTURY BACKGROUND

1. Alfred H. Barr, Jr., *Matisse—His Art and His Public* (New York, 1951), p. 86.

2. *Ibid.*, p. 82.

3. Henry van de Velde, "Der Neue Stil" (from *Vom neuen Stil*, 1907), in *Zum neuen Stil: Aus seinen Schriften ausgewählt und eingeleitet von Hans Curjel* (Munich, 1955), p. 156. (All writings by Van de Velde are quoted from this source.) Van de Velde preferred to speak of "Neue Stil" and "Moderne Stil" rather than "Jugendstil."

4. Van de Velde, "Prinzipielle Erklärungen" (from *Kunstgewerbliche Laienpredigten*, 1902), *ibid.*, p. 116.

5. Quoted in Barr, *op. cit.*, p. 118.

6. Van de Velde, "Das Neue Ornament" (from *Die Renaissance im Kunstgewerbe*, 1901), *op. cit.*, p. 101.

7. Yvonne Thirion, "L'Influence de l'estampe japonaise dans l'oeuvre de Gauguin," *Gazette des Beaux-Arts* (1958), p. 95.

Ingres, whom Gauguin admired, employed in *The Bather of Valpinçon* (1808, Louvre) a similarly ambivalent background plane.

8. John Rewald, *Post-Impressionism—From Van Gogh to Gauguin* (New York, 1956), p. 201.

9. From a letter to Van Gogh, September 1888, first published by Rewald, *ibid.*, p. 202.

10. Werner Hofmann, *Das Irdische Paradise: Kunst im 19. Jahrhundert* (Munich, 1960), pp. 233, 331. (English edition, *The Earthly Paradise: Art in the Nineteenth Century* [New York, 1961].)

11. Quoted in Van de Velde, "Déblaiement d'Art," *op. cit.*, p. 23.

12. Félix Fénéon, *Au-delà de l'Impressionnisme* (Paris, 1966), p. 141; André Chastel, "Une Source oubliée de Seurat," *Archives de l'Art français*, N.P., XXII (1959), 400; Charles Henry, *Cercle Chromatique*, Paris, 1889.

13. *Bonnard, Vuillard et les Nabis (1888–1903)* (Paris, Musée National d'Art Moderne, 1955), p. 78.

14. *Picasso* (London, Tate Gallery, 1960), p. 17.
The "picture within the picture" belongs to the as yet unexplored preliminary stages of collage technique, as does the *Mehrfeld-Bild* (Hans H. Hofstätter, *Symbolismus und die Kunst der Jahrhundertwende* [Cologne, 1965], p. 121). Surprisingly, André Chastel in his lecture on "Le tableau dans le tableau" has completely overlooked this aspect (*Akten des 21. Internationalen Kongresses für Kunstgeschichte in Bonn*, 1964, I [Berlin, 1967], 15).

15. Günther Bandmann, *Picasso: Les Demoiselles d'Avignon* (Stuttgart, 1965) (No. 109 in the series *Werkmonographien zur bildenden Kunst*). The Musée des Beaux-Arts at Rouen possesses a *Diana Bathing* by François Clouet (reproduced in the catalogue of the exhibition *Le 16ᵉ siècle européen* [Paris, Petit Palais, 1965/66], No. 74) comparable to Picasso's pictorial concept.

16. Peter Selz and Mildred Constantine, eds., *Art Nouveau: Art and Design at the Turn of the Century* (New York, 1959), p. 83.
Such alternating affinities are also met in pictures dating from the beginnings of the panel picture, where remainders of abstract pictorial arrangement have survived. A fine example is Pisanello's *Vision of St. Eustache* (London, National Gallery); the scroll pro-

[246]

vides an abstract "commentary" on the movement of the dog in the foreground.

17. L. de Marshalle (E. L. Kirchner), "Zeichnungen von E. L. Kirchner," in *Genius* (1920), p. 216, as quoted by Lothar-Günther Buchheim, *Die Künstlergemeinschaft Brücke* (Feldafing, 1956), p. 162.

18. Quoted in *Brücke, 1905–1913, Eine Künstlergemeinschaft der Expressionismus* (Essen, Museum Folkwang, 1958), pp. 24, 28.

19. Oskar Kokoschka, *Die Träumenden Knaben und andere Dichtungen* (Salzburg, 1959), p. 24. An as yet unremarked literary parallel to *Die Träumenden Knaben* exists in Robert Musil's tale *Die Verwirrungen des Zöglings Törless*, 1906.

20. *Ibid.*, p. 26.

21. Oskar Kokoschka, *Der Expressionismus Edvard Munchs* (Vienna, 1953), p. 23.

22. Vincent van Gogh, *Sämtliche Briefe* (Berlin, 1965), IV, 139. (English edition, *The Collected Letters of Vincent van Gogh*, 3 vols. [New York, 1958].)

23. Alma Mahler, *Mein Leben* (Frankfurt am Main, 1960), p. 130. Entry dated March 25, 1919.

24. Ernst H. Gombrich, "Visual Metaphors of Value in Art," in *Symbols and Values: An Initial Study*, 13th Symposium of the Conference on Science, Philosophy and Religion (New York, 1954).

25. Robert Schmutzler, *Art Nouveau* (New York, 1962), ills. 105 and 106.

26. Dante, *The Inferno*, Canto V (trans. H. W. Longfellow).

27. From the *Messaggio* in the catalogue of the Nuove Tendenze group's first exhibition (Milan, 1914), reproduced in the catalogue of the permanent Sant'Elia exhibition (Como, 1962), p. 121. Recently Peter Wolf has drawn attention to Eugène Hénard (1849–1923), "the first modern urbanist," who was architect of the city of Paris from 1900 to 1914. According to Wolf, "Futurism, through F. T. Marinetti (Antonio Sant'Elia's principal informer), gathered inspiration from Hénard" (*The Architectural Forum*, Vol. 127 [October, 1967], p. 50).

28. Van de Velde, "Aperçus en vue d'une synthèse d'art," *op. cit.,* p. 37.

The Vienna Secession's declaration of principles also alluded to the symbolic preeminence of the tower: "We would teach you, in union with us, to become stable like a tower of brass because you perceive, know, understand, are initiates and masters over the spirits! Let this be our mission!" (*Ver Sacrum,* 1898, p. 7.)

29. Christa Baumgart, *Geschichte des Futurismus* (Reinbek bei Hamburg, 1966), p. 182. Joshua C. Taylor, *Futurism* (New York, 1961), p. 126.

30. Joshua C. Taylor, *ibid.,* p. 124.

31. Van de Velde, "Gedankenfolge für einen Vortag" (from *Notizen aus Griechenland,* 1903), *op. cit.,* p. 135.

32. "The frank, commanding beauty of the individual parts of the machines has to have been deeply felt—those enormous machines, which load the electric accumulators with solemn, consecratory manner, in order to appreciate the divine harmony and perfect rhythm of the Parthenon." (Van de Velde, "Der Neue Stil" [from *Vom neuen Stil,* 1907], *op. cit.,* p. 165).

33. Van de Velde, "Aperçus en vue d'une synthèse d'art," *op. cit.,* p. 55.

34. Quoted in Baumgart, *op. cit.,* pp. 28–29, and Taylor, *op. cit.,* p. 125. Marinetti's first epic poem (1902) was called *The Conquest of the Stars.*

35. Carrà wrote in 1913, "The depiction of tones, noises, and aromas demands . . . zigzag and wavy lines. . . ." (Baumgart, *op. cit.,* p. 186.)

36. Rainer Maria Rilke, *Rodin* (Leipzig, 1920), p. 117.

37. Though void of any intellectual depth whatever, art of the hackneyed and *salon* sort also takes into account the theme of soaring-up-and-away. Among the most famous was William Adolphe Bouguereau's *Les Oréades,* 1902.

38. Stanislaw Przybyszewski as quoted by Gösta Svenaeus, *Trädet pa berget, En Studie i förhallendet Munch-Nietzsche* (Arbok, 1963), p. 32. Also by the same author, *Idé och innehall i Edvard Munchs Konst* (Oslo, 1953). Mr. Pal Hougen, Curator of Oslo's Munch

Museet, has drawn my attention to the relationship between *Menschenberg* and Ibsen's *When We Dead Awake* (1899) in which the sculptor Rubek is credited with a similar composition.

39. Van de Velde, "Säuberung der Kunst" (from "Déblaiement d'Art," 1894), *op. cit.*, p. 35.

40. Maurice Denis, "Du Symbolisme au Classicisme," *Théories, 1890–1910* (Paris, 1964), p. 61.

41. Paul Gauguin, *Lettres à sa femme et à ses amis*, Maurice Malingue, ed. (Paris, 1946), p. 45. (English edition, *Paul Gauguin, Letters to His Wife and Friends* [Cleveland, 1949].)

42. Heinrich Wölfflin, "Prolegomena zu einer Psychologie der Architektur," *Kleine Schriften* (Basel, 1946), p. 20.

43. That the psychic relevance of formal contents is subject to limitations is evinced by Lichtenberg's penetrating criticism of Lavater's physiognomy (see Werner Hofmann, *Grundlagen der Modernen Kunst* [Stuttgart, 1966], p. 250.)

44. This momentous concept, whose ambiguity cannot be discussed here, was coined by the Viennese art historian Alois Riegl in his work *Stilfragen* (Berlin, 1893).

45. Denis, *op. cit.*, p. 43. Regarding the abstract appreciation of pictures, see Otto Stelzer, *Die Vorgeschichte der abstrakten Kunst. Denkmodelle und Vor-Bilder* (Munich, 1964), and Hofmann, *Grundlagen der Modernen Kunst*, p. 166.

46. Denis, *op. cit.*, p. 48.

47. Michel Seuphor, *Piet Mondrian: Life and Work* (New York, n.d.), p. 117.

48. Chastel, *op. cit.*, p. 400; Hofmann, *The Earthly Paradise*, p. 131.

49. Adolf Loos, "Ornament und Verbrechen" (1908), in *Sämtliche Schriften in Zwei Bänden* (Vienna, 1962), I, 277.
Stanislaw Przybyszewski, in *Totenmesse* (1895), sought to abrogate the dualism of spirit and nature, man and woman: "I see nature as an apocalyptic apotheosis of the eternally raised phallus which with exorbitantly gross waste pours floods of semen over the universe" (Svenaeus, *op. cit.*, p. 31). The cosmic implications of the perpendicular were already intimated by Charles Blanc (*Grammaire des Arts du Dessin* [Paris, 1867]), who enunciated that

[249]

through the body of an upright human there runs an axis whose beginning lies at the earth's center and which reaches into the firmament (Chastel, *op. cit.*, p. 403).

50. "Natural appearance disguises the expression of the affinities" (quoted in Seuphor, *op. cit.*, p. 304).

51. Reprinted in Ewald Bender, *Die Kunst des Ferdinand Hodlers* (Zurich, 1923), p. 201.

52. Werner Hofmann, "Zu einem Bildmittel Edvard Munchs," in *Alte und neue Kunst* (1954), p. 20; Klaus Lankheit, *Das Triptychon als Pathosformel* (Heidelberg, 1959), p. 61.

53. For the iconographic background, see Hofmann, *The Earthly Paradise*, and Hans H. Hofstätter, *Symbolismus und die Kunst der Jahrhundertwende* (Cologne, 1965). The examples cited there should be complemented by Kupka's *Autumn Sun* (1906) in the Musée National d'Art Moderne, Paris (*Inventaire de l'Oeuvre de Kupka* [Paris, 1966], No. 16) and Kolo Moser's *Three Women* (c. 1904) in the Museum des 20. Jahrhunderts, Vienna. In his opera *Siberia* (1903), Umberto Giordano conceived the three acts like parts of a triptych: "La donna" (first act), "L'amante" (second act), "L'eroina" (third act).

54. Selz and Constantine, *op. cit.*, p. 72.
    On Toorop's painting, see Ludwig Hevesi, *Acht Jahre Sezession* (Vienna, 1906), p. 241. Chekhov's *Three Sisters* (1901) offers a psychological differentiation of the female triptych. Chekhov was interested in Ibsen and perhaps also in Munch, who exhibited as early as 1897 in St. Petersburg (this information is from Reinhold A. Heller).

55. Seuphor, *op. cit.*, p. 315.

56. Mondrian, quoted in *ibid.*, p. 322.

57. For example, productions of *Hamlet*, 1908, and *Electra*, 1905. See also Ferruccio Marotti, "Appia e Craig—le origini della scena moderna" in *La Biennale di Venezia* (1963), No. 50/51, pp. 43, 48.

58. Seuphor, *op. cit.*, p. 312.

59. *Munich 1869–1958—Dawn of Modern Art Exhibition* (Munich, Haus der Kunst, 1958), Figs. 250–255, 260–261.

60. Denis, *op. cit.*, p. 40.
    In 1910 Kandinsky, in *Über das Geistige in der Kunst* (Berne,

1952, p. 51), called Matisse "one of the greatest of the French moderns" but distinguished between pictures possessing the sanction of "inner necessity"—a favorite concept with Kandinsky—and such as had "in the main or exclusively only external life." (English edition, *On the Spiritual in Art* [New York, 1946].)

61. Will Grohmann, *Kandinsky* (Cologne, 1958), p. 35. (English edition, *Kandinsky* [New York, 1958].)

62. By virtue of his chairmanship of the Phalanx art group, Kandinsky in 1904 arranged for the exhibition at Munich of pictures by Signac and Rysselberghe (Grohmann, *ibid.*, p. 36).

63. Examples of different pitches of expression are furnished by Arnold Böcklin, *Ruggiero and Angelica* and *The Adventurer*; Louis Corinth, *Perseus and Andromeda*; Jean Dampt, *The Beautiful Melusine* (reproduced in *Pan*, 1895, 2nd issue); Georges de Fenre, *Tales*; Rudolf Henneberg, *The Pursuit of Happiness*; Klimt, *Beethoven-Fries* and *Das Leben ein Kampf*; Kokoschka, *Ritter, Tod und Engel*; Picasso, *Evocation*; Redon, *The Green Horse, Saint George*; Hans Thoma, *The Keeper of the Valley*; Heinrich Vogeler, *The Frog King*.

64. Quoted by Johannes Eichner in *Kandinsky und Gabriele Munter. Von Ursprüngen moderner Kunst* (Munich, 1957), p. 115.

65. *Ibid.*, p. 116.

66. Two proto-Fauvist early works of Vlaminck, *Le Père Bouju* (1900) and *Sur le Zinc* (1900, *Ill. 88*), anticipate this process.

67. Denis, *op. cit.*, p. 57.

68. Henri Matisse, *Farbe und Gleichnis—Gesammelte Schriften* (Zurich, 1955), p. 27. (Original French published as "Notes d'un Peintre" in *La Grande Revue* [December 25, 1908].) Quoted in Barr, *op. cit.*, p. 122.

69. Sir Joshua Reynolds, *Discourses on Art* (New York, 1961), p. 50. (Discourse Three, delivered to the Students of the Royal Academy, on the distribution of the prizes, December 14, 1770).

III: NEGATIVE BEAUTY

1. Daniel-Henry Kahnweiler, *Les Sculptures de Picasso* (Paris, 1949), pl. 6.

2. Ill. John Rewald, *Post-Impressionism—From Van Gogh to Gau-*

guin (New York, 1956), pp. 253 and 290. Compare these Gauguin postures with the woman on the right upper corner of Bernard's *Bathers* (*Ill. 146*), which was probably shown in the Café Volpini Exhibition, 1889. The smoother, more Art Nouveau version of the crouched figure is exemplified by the French sculptor Fix Masseau's *Emprise* (reproduced in *Pan*, 1895, p. 135), which already points in the direction of Maillol's *La Nuit* (1909).

3. Maillol effected the return of the seated pose from the "vulgar" to the classic realm. In doing so, he was in harmony with Hippolyte Flandrin's *Young Man on the Sea-Shore* (1855, Louvre), a highly popular nineteenth-century picture. It is conceivable that Flandrin inspired Maillol.

4. Gauguin, *La Femme du Roi*, 1896, Pushkin Museum, Moscow.

5. The "circling werewolf" mentioned in *Die Träumenden Knaben* (Salzburg, 1959) in these drawings assumed shape. The key to Kokoschka's analytical portraits, starting in 1909, is also to be sought in that work. These depictions give the impression of stripping and gashing their subjects. The poem had already proclaimed, " . . . my body enhanced with blood and hue . . . crawls into your souls, festers in your bodies. . . . " (p. 16).

6. Léon Bloy passed negative judgment on Rouault's interpretation: "His [Rouault's] reaction to middle class baseness is so gruesome that his art seems mortally wounded by it. He set out to depict my Poulots, but I don't want to have anything to do with illustrations of that kind. He transforms two ordinary middle class individuals into a couple of petty suburban criminals." (Quoted in Pierre Courthion, *Georges Rouault* [Cologne, 1962], p. 103. English edition, *Georges Rouault* [New York, n.d.].)

7. Letter to Fritz Winter, May 3, 1929 (as stated in a letter by Dr. Ludwig Grote). See also Eberhard Roters, "E. L. Kirchner's Begriff der 'Hieroglyphe' und die Bedeutung des graphischen Details," in *Festschrift für E. Redslob* (Berlin, 1955). Étienne Boullée (1728–99) had already proposed that winter should be depicted by way of rigorous, angular contours and the pleasanter seasons by flowing forms (*Boullée's Treatise on Architecture*, Helen Rosenau, ed. [London, 1953], p. 43).

8. Peter Selz and Mildred Constantine, eds., *Art Nouveau: Art and Design at the Turn of the Century* (New York, 1959), p. 83.

9. Françoise Gilot and Carlton Lake, *Life with Picasso* (New York, 1964), pp. 75–76.

10. Quoted in Alfred H. Barr, Jr., *Matisse—His Art and His Public* (New York, 1951), p. 551.

11. Walter Crane, *Line and Form* (London, 1902) (1st edition, 1900), p. 103.

12. Crane's two systems can be traced back into the nineteenth century. In his novel *Der Grüne Heinrich*, Gottfried Keller describes the drawing lessons his hero takes with an old artist who tells him what he had learned around 1780 in Dresden: according to the two categories of trees—those with crenate and those with round foliage—there are only two methods of drawing, the crenate oak manner and the rounded linden manner. See also Jean Paul's *Vorschule der Ästhetik*, XIV Program, section 79.

13. Henry R. Hope, *Georges Braque* (New York, 1949), p. 21.

14. Figured bass is a system of accompaniment in which the bass line is written out all "through" the composition, but its harmonization is left to the accompanist to provide more or less impromptu. Figures added to the bass line inform the accompanist as to the harmony resulting from the melodic part he is accompanying so that his own harmonization will not conflict with it.

15. Barr, *op. cit.*, p. 87.

16. Émile Bernard, "Souvenirs sur Paul Cezanne et lettres inédites," *Mercure de France* (October, 1907), p. 400.

17. Daniel-Henry Kahnweiler, *Der Weg zum Kubismus* (new edition, Stuttgart, 1958), p. 37. (English edition, *The Rise of Cubism* [New York, 1949].)

18. *Ibid.*, p. 74.
   In the eighteenth century, when a start was made with the establishment of schematic sign alphabets, two trends revealed themselves. The first employed irregular abbreviations (Hogarth, *The Analysis of Beauty*, 1753, table II, fig. 71); the other let the multitude of perceptual objects emanate from a limited number of regular figures (Gérard de Lairesse, *Les Principes du Dessein* . . .

[Amsterdam, 1719], pp. 6, 7). Bernardin de Saint-Pierre traced all forms back to the straight line, the triangle, the circle, the ellipse and the parabola and took the view that all natural forms could once more be derived therefrom (*Études de la Nature*, Vol. 2 [Paris, 1784], p. 122).

19. Hofmann, *Grundlagen der Modernen Kunst* (Stuttgart, 1966), p. 71.

20. Christopher Gray, *Cubist Aesthetic Theories* (Baltimore, 1953), p. 50; Guillaume Apollinaire, *The Cubist Painters—Aesthetic Meditations* (1913)—*Documents of Modern Art 1* (New York, 1962), p. 18. On the productive misinterpretation of Cézanne on the part of the Cubists, see Hofmann, *Grundlagen der Modernen Kunst*, p. 276.

21. Spontaneity, too, is tied to convention and rule. (See Ernst H. Gombrich, *Art and Illusion* [London, 1960], p. 173.)

22. Henry van de Velde, "Vom neuen Stil" 1901), in *Zum neuen Stil: Aus seinen Schriften ausgewählt und eingeleitet von Hans Curjel* (Munich, 1955), p. 89. In 1895 Van de Velde discerned in ornamentation "the sole true source of art" and demanded of painting and sculpture that they should return "to their most truly inherent trait of being ornamental" ("Aperçus en vue d'une synthèse d'art," *op. cit.*, p. 50). In his book *Die Renaissance im Kunstgewerbe* (1901) and in his *Kunstgewerblichen Laienpredigten* (1902) (*op. cit.*, pp. 94, 128) he once more spoke up on behalf of ornamentation. These sentiments explain why Loos fought Van de Velde as ornamentation's most prominent defender.

23. "We have a bad habit of trying to disguise disagreeable necessities by some form of sudden decoration. . . ." (John Ruskin, *The Seven Lamps of Architecture* [New York, 1853], Chptrs. IV, XXI, XXII).

24. Louis Sullivan, "Ornament in Architecture," in *Kindergarten Chats and Other Writings—Documents of Modern Art 4* (New York, 1947), p. 187.

25. Adolf Loos, "Das Luxusfuhrwerk," in *Sämtliche Schriften in Zwei Bänden* (Vienna, 1962) , I, 65.

26. Adolf Loos, "Ornament und Verbrechen," *ibid.*, p. 277.

27. Adolf Loos, from his periodical *Das andere* (1903), *ibid.*, p. 241.

28. Van de Velde, "Das Neue Ornament" (from *Die Renaissance im Kunstgewerbe*, 1901), *op. cit.*, p. 101.

29. Adolf Loos, *Von einem armen reichen Mann*, *ibid.*, p. 202.

30. Gustav Künstler and Ludwig Münz, *Der Architekt Adolf Loos* (Vienna, 1964), pp. 51, 83, 84–85. (English edition, *Adolf Loos, Pioneer of Modern Architecture* [New York, 1966].)

31. Ruskin, *op. cit.*, preface to the second edition (1855). Loos, *op. cit.*, p. 315.

32. Adolf Loos, from *Das andere*, *op. cit.*, p. 240. Written in 1903, this challenge could well have been inspired by Munch's death scenes.

33. Van de Velde, "Das Neue Ornament," *op. cit.*, p. 101.

34. Friedrich Nietzsche, "Die Freier der Wirklichkeit," *Menschliches, Allzumenschliches*, II, Chptr. 3.

35. According to the prevailing building regulations houses were permitted to have above the ground-floor "only an attic in the roof zone" (Künstler and Münz, *op. cit.*, p. 75) .

36. Kahnweiler, *op. cit.*, p. 40.

37. *Ibid.*, p. 52.

38. Wassily Kandinsky, "Über die Formfrage," in Klaus Lankheit, ed., *Der Blaue Reiter* (Munich, 1965), p. 143.

39. It seems hardly likely that Kandinsky would have been familiar with Ruskin's counterparts, "art without facts" and "facts without art." (On Ruskin, see Hofmann, *Grundlagen der Modernen Kunst*, p. 166.)

40. Lankheit, *op. cit.*, p. 279.

41. Wilhelm Worringer, *Abstraktion und Einfühlung* (Munich, 1921, eleventh edition), p. 21. Original edition, 1908. (English edition, *Abstraction and Empathy* [London, 1953].)

42. Alois Riegl, *Die Spätrömische Kunstindustrie*, 1901 (reprinted, Vienna, 1929). Too little attention has been paid to the publication, in the same year as Riegl's original edition, of Schlosser's essay "Zur Genesis der mittelalterlichen Kunstanschauung." Its effort to rehabilitate so-called epochs of decay in no way lags behind Riegl's, and indeed perhaps surpasses it in perspicuity and psychological insight. A reprint is to be found in *Präludien* (Berlin, 1927), p. 180.

43. Riegl, *ibid.*, p. 90; Worringer, *op. cit.*, p. 122.

44. Riegl, *ibid.*, p. 124.

45. *Ibid.*, p. 49; Worringer, *op. cit.*, p. 124.

46. Quoted in Lankheit, *op. cit.*, p. 148.

IV: *LAWFUL BEAUTY AND TRUTH TO LIFE*

1. Ludwig Hevesi, *Altkunst—Neukunst* (Vienna, 1909), p. 313.

2. The Russian contribution to the theme of this book has not been included here because, despite the excellent description in Camilla Gray's *The Great Experiment: Russian Art 1863–1922* (New York, 1962), it has still been investigated only in part. Insofar as its evolution can be assessed, this corresponds roughly to the western European polarization between Dadaism and Constructivism.

3. It seems improbable that there were any contacts between these artists. *Cf.* Kandinsky's testimony in a letter to Hans Hildebrandt, printed in *Werk* (October, 1955), p. 329.

4. Maurice Denis, "Définition du Néo-Traditionnisme," *Art et Critique* (August 23 and 30, 1890). Reprinted in *Théories* [Paris, 1920], p. 1.)

5. Wassily Kandinsky, "Über die Formfrage," in Klaus Lankheit, ed., *Der Blaue Reiter* (Munich, 1965), p. 154.

6. The Russian Malevich was among those who explored the geometric purification of the pictorial space to its uttermost limits (Ill. 108). I have, however, refrained from including this pioneer contribution into the context of this study since it is still somewhat obscured by the fact that important sources in the U.S.S.R. are inaccessible. Furthermore, a recent publication indicates that Malevich in later years made kinds of replicas of his earlier works and dated them "1910," etc. (El Lissitzky, *Maler Architekt Typograf Fotograf* [Dresden, 1967], p. 88).

7. Kandinsky, *op. cit.*, p. 148.

8. The spread of Cubism has been described by Robert Rosenblum in his book *Cubism and the Twentieth Century* (New York, 1960).

9. Christa Baumgart, *Geschichte des Futurismus* (Reinbek bei Hamburg, 1966), pp. 81, 204.

10. *Ibid.*, p. 86.

11. *Ibid.*, p. 31.

[256]

12. Guillaume Apollinaire, *The Cubist Painters—Aesthetic Meditations* (1913)—*Documents of Modern Art 1* (New York, 1962), p. 10.

13. Quoted by Camilla Gray, *op. cit.*, p. 124.

14. Daniel-Henry Kahnweiler, *Der weg zum Kubismus* (new edition, Stuttgart, 1958), p. 102. (English edition, *The Rise of Cubism* [New York, 1949].)

15. That letters can be alienated from their function lies outside the one-dimensional perceptive convention. (*Cf.* John Ruskin on the letters of the alphabet in *The Seven Lamps of Architecture* [New York, 1853], Chptr. IV, Sec. IX.) The Calligramme drawings by Apollinaire (first published in *Calligrammes* [Paris, 1918]) can be traced back to medieval manuscripts (see Fritz Saxl, *Illuminated Science Manuscripts in England*, in *Lectures* [London, 1957], I, 96; II, Pl. 58a.)

16. For the history of their organization, see Lankheit, *op. cit.*, p. 253.

17. On the occasion of the memorial exhibition *European Art 1912* (Cologne, Wallraf Richartz Museum, 1962) the catalogue of the Sonderbund exhibition was photo-mechanically reproduced.

18. Milton W. Brown, *The Story of the Armory Show* (New York, 1963).

19. Catalogue of the exhibition *Der Sturm—Herwarth Walden und die Europäische Avantgarde, Berlin 1912–1932* (Berlin, National-galerie, 1961).

20. Apollinaire, however, compared Gris with Ingres and David, Picabia with Poussin (*op. cit.*, pp. 42, 46).

21. Apollinaire provided a justification for the sculptor Duchamp-Villon by references to the Assyrians, the Egyptians, and Negroid and Oceanic art (*ibid.*, p. 48).

22. Roberto Papini, *Lacerba*, I (January 1, 1913), quoted in *Archivi del Futurismo* (Rome, 1958), pp. 130–133.

23. Friedrich Nietzsche, "Gegen die Kunst der Kunstwerke," *Menschliches, Allzumenschliches*, II, 174.

24. Quoted by Baumgart, *op. cit.*, p. 199. Joshua C. Taylor, *Futurism* (New York, 1961), p. 133.

25. Apollinaire, with his allusions to mosaic-workers' "paint with marble or colored wood," already gave intimation of the as yet

[257]

continuing uninvestigated prehistory of multimateriality (*op. cit.*, p. 23).

26. Kandinsky, *op. cit.*, p. 157.

27. Alfred Kubin, *Die andere Seite* (Munich, 1962), p. 103, first published in 1909. (English edition, *The Other Side* [New York, 1967].)

Did Kandinsky know Kubin's novel? The question can be raised since Kubin was a member of the Blue Rider group of 1911.

28. Kandinsky, *op. cit.*, p. 161.

29. *Ibid.*

30. *Ibid.*

31. Kurt Schwitters, "Die Merzmalerei," in *Der Cicerone* (1919), p. 582. MERZ was a variety of Dadaist art. Schwitters derived the term from the arbitrary fragmentation of the word KOMMERZ.

32. Kasimir Malevich, *Die Gegenstandslose Welt* (Munich, 1927), p. 196.

33. Calvin Tomkins quotes Robert Rauschenberg's statement: "I don't think Duchamp meant any of his things to be just gestures. . . . His *Bicycle Wheel* has always struck me as one of the most beautiful pieces I've ever seen." (*The Bride and the Bachelors* [New York, 1965], p. 236.)

34. Marcel Duchamp, *Marchand du Sel* (Paris, 1958), p. 112.

35. Nietzsche's rejection of false idealists coincides with Duchamp's derision of "generalizations" (Duchamp, *ibid.*, p. 12).

36. The manuscript was completed in 1910 and was published, with the date 1912, in December, 1911. (See Max Bill, Introduction to the fourth German edition, *Über das Geistige in der Kunst* [Berne-Dumpliz, 1952]; English edition, *On the Spiritual in Art* [New York, 1947].)

37. Wilhelm Worringer had already observed the connection between Gothic and engineering architecture: "A degree of inner comprehension of Gothic had to await modern iron construction art when there once more occurred the case of artistic expression being attained by the constructional means themselves." This affinity nevertheless undergoes some qualifications by reason of his remark that engineering architecture is not based on a new

will to form but simply on a new material (*Formprobleme der Gotik* [Munich, 1912], p. 72; English edition, *Form in Gothic* [New York, 1964]).

38. There is an affinity between Mondrian's *Composition with Trees II* (1912–1913, *Ill. 64*) and Duchamp's *Sad Young Man in a Train* (1911, *Ill. 123*).

39. Worringer, *op. cit.*

40. Duchamp, *op. cit.*, p. 111. In his "Natural and Abstract Reality" (1919/20), Mondrian holds the painter's subjective handwriting responsible for universality remaining disguised in older art (Michel Seuphor, *Piet Mondrian: Life and Work* [New York, n.d.], p. 341).

41. Duchamp, *op. cit.*, p. 154. In the New Configuration the "personal factor" is reduced to vanishing point; only when "individual emotions" are silent, can the "universal sensibility" be determined (Seuphor, *ibid.*, p. 342).

42. Quoted in Seuphor, *ibid.*, p. 118.

43. Henry van de Velde, "Ein Kapitel über Entwurf und Bau moderner Möbel" (from *Pan*, 1897), *Zum neuen Stil: Aus seinen Schriften ausgewählt und eingeleitet von Hans Curjel* (Munich, 1955), p. 59.

44. Van de Velde, "Säuberung der Kunst" (from "Déblaiement d'Art," 1894), *ibid.*, p. 27.

45. Apollinaire, *op. cit.*, p. 14.

46. H. C. L. Jaffé, *De Stijl 1917–1931* (Amsterdam, 1956), p. 85.

47. Quoted by Seuphor, *op. cit.*, p. 137.

48. *Ibid.*, p. 141.

49. "The time will come when we will be able to dispense with all the arts as we know them today; then ripened beauty will be tangible reality" (both quoted by Seuphor, *op. cit.*, p. 341).

50. *Ibid.*, p. 326.

51. *Ibid.*, p. 337.

52. *Ibid.*, p. 339.

53. *Ibid.*

54. Van de Velde had enunciated, "Man can attain beauty without art" ("Die Belebung des Stoffes als Prinzip der Schönheit" [from *Essays*, 1910], *op. cit.*, p. 172).

55. Albert Camus, *Oeuvres*, II (Paris, Edition de la Pléiade 1967), 658.

56. Piet Mondrian, *Plastic Art and Pure Plastic Art—Documents of Modern Art 2* (New York, 1945), p. 32.

57. Seuphor, *op. cit.*, p. 321.

58. William Morris, *The Decorative Arts* (Boston, 1878). This outlook anticipated Mondrian's rejection of luxury (see above, note 53).

59. John Ruskin, *The Stones of Venice* (New York and London, 1851–1853), III, Chptr. IV, Sec. VI. Duchamp, too, was conscious of the emptiness of the conventional qualitative notion of art and had sought the extension of it to "bad art" (*op. cit.*, p. 168).

60. Quoted in Seuphor, *op. cit.*, p. 117.

61. Ruskin, *The Stones of Venice*, II, Chptr. VI, Secs. XLII–XLIII. Duchamp accepts the multimateriality postulated by Kandinsky most surely when Kandinsky says, "An artist might use anything—a dot, a line, the most conventional or unconventional symbol—to say what he wants to say" (*op. cit.*, p. 111). Subject matter for a philosophic discussion is whether undisguised "truth to life," which is the gain of "artlessness," accords with the merit of the "mere thing," which Hegel contrasts with a work of art's "soulful form." Hegel circumscribes the spiritual merit of the sensuous-beautiful and leaves it to religion to satisfy its need for effigy outside the sphere of the work of art:

"It is one thing for the mind to have before it a mere thing—such as the Host *per se*, a piece of stone or wood, or a wretched daub; quite another thing for it to contemplate a painting, rich in thought and sentiment, or a beautiful work of sculpture, in looking at which soul holds converse with soul and spirit with spirit. In the former case, spirit is torn from its proper element, bound to something utterly alien to it—the sensuous, the unspiritual. In the latter, on the contrary, the sensuous object is a beautiful one, and the spiritual form with which it is endued gives it a soul and contains truth in itself. But on the one hand, this element of truth as thus exhibited is manifested only in a sensuous mode, not in its appropriate form; on the other hand, while religion normally involves independence of that which is essentially a mere outward and material object—a mere thing—that kind of religion which is now under consideration finds no satisfaction in being brought into connection with the beautiful; the coarsest, ugliest, poorest representations will suit its purpose equally well—perhaps better. . . . Thus art in its very nature transcended the principle of the Church" (*Philosophy of History*, Part IV, Sec. II, Chptr. 3, Sub-Sec. "Art and Science as Putting a Period to the Middle Ages"). The foregoing should be compared with the controversy between C. D. Friedrich and Ramdohr about the "Tetschener Altar" (Werner Hofmann, "Bemerkungen zum Tetschener Altar von C. D. Friedrich," in *Christliche Kunstblätter*, No. 2 [1962], p. 50).

62. Werner Hofmann, *Caricature from Leonardo to Picasso* (London, 1956).

63. Quoted in James Thrall Soby, *Giorgio de Chirico* (New York, 1955), p. 251.

64. *Ibid.*, p. 67.

65. Kandinsky, *op. cit.*, p. 168.

66. *Ibid.*, p. 169.

67. Duchamp, *op. cit.*, p. 16.

68. This goes so far that recently he had even agreed to the reproduction and commercialization of his ready-mades (*L'Oeil* [May, 1967].)

69. Quoted in Hans Richter, *Dada—Kunst und Antikunst* (Cologne, 1965), p. 30. (English edition, *Dada—Art and Anti-Art* [New York, 1965], p. 32.)

70. Multiple value of form is one of the intrinsic hallmarks of caricature. The classic evidence for this characteristic is furnished by the speech of defense made by the French newspaper publisher Philipon when his pear-shaped caricatures of King Louis-Philippe involved him in civil proceedings. (See Hofmann, *Caricature from Leonardo to Picasso*, p. 31). Significant for the interest aroused by modern art in caricature's abstract-linear qualities is Worringer's aphorism, "This passage into one another of the line characteristic of reality and the autonomous line following only its own expression is seen most clearly in caricature" (*op. cit.*, p. 42). Hugo von Hofmannsthal was the first to extol caricature's capacity to

"perceive things, regardless of their conventional meaning, as form *per se*" (Franz Stuck, 1894, in *Prosa*, I [Frankfurt am Main, 1950], 170).

71. Tristan Tzara, quoted by Richter, *op. cit.*, p. 169.

72. Baumgart, *op. cit.*, p. 148; Richter, *ibid.*, p. 18.

73. Quoted by Richter, *ibid.*, p. 49.

74. Hans Arp, *Unsern täglichen Traum* (Zurich, 1955), p. 74.

75. Quoted in François Ruchon, *Jules Laforgue* (Geneva, 1924), p. 55. In an essay "on the beauty of ugly pictures," which uses a motto from Laforgue, the Prague writer Max Brod declares himself capable to decipher "the chaos of primitive rituals from commercial ads, postage stamps, transfer pictures, etc. . . ." and concludes: "I am enchanted by the Romanticism of the tasteless." This essay was published for the first time in 1913, i.e., parallel with—but certainly without information about—the Cubist "collages" (new edition, Max Brod, *Über die Schönheit hässlicher Bilder* [Vienna, 1967]).

76. Hofmann, *Grundlagen der Modernen Kunst* (Stuttgart, 1966), p. 202.

77. " . . . senza elettione delle megliori forme naturali, quello che à dire è stupendo, pare che senz'arte emulasse l'arte" (Giovanni Pietro Bellori, *Le Vite de' pittori, scultori et architetti moderni*, 1672, p. 201). Bellori was probably the first modern theoretician to recognize the "formlessness" of realism, subsequently ever and again reviled by the idealistic camp. "Artlessness" derives its origin in part from this source (Hofmann, *ibid.*, pp. 164, 343).

78. Arp, *op. cit.*, p. 50.

79. Richter, *op. cit.*, p. 57. For Dada and the overall work of art, see pp. 34, 38, 155.

80. Arp, *op. cit.*, p. 50.

V: TOWARD THE ART OF ARTLESSNESS

1. Louis H. Sullivan, *Kindergarten Chats and Other Writings— Documents of Modern Art 4* (New York, 1947), p. 45.

2. Odilon Redon, *A Soi-Même* (Journal, 1867–1915), (Paris, 1961), p. 100.

[262]

3. Illustrated in Catalogue of the Secession Exhibition, *Europäische Kunst um die Jahrhundertwende* (Munich, 1964), Ill. I (Hofmann); Catalogue of the Neue Galerie des Kunsthistorischen Museums (Vienna, 1966), Ill. 13 (Klinger).

4. Quoted in Peter Selz and Mildred Constantine, eds., *Art Nouveau: Art and Design at the Turn of the Century* (New York, 1959), p. 77.

5. O. H. A. Schmitz, "Die Abendröte der Kunst," *Pan* (Berlin, 1898), 4th issue, p. 188.
The text leaves it open whether the author in his reference to "material" meant a work's fabric or subject.

6. Henry-Russell Hitchcock, *Gaudi* (New York, 1957), *passim*.

7. Ludwig Hevesi, *Acht Jahre Secession* (Vienna, 1906), p. 193.
This concept was reinvented by El Lissitzky in the twenties.

8. The term "disturbed form" has originated with Ernst H. Gombrich ("Zum Werke Giulio Romanos," *Jahrbuch der kunsthistorischen Sammlungen in Wien*, NF VIII/IX [1934/35]).

9. Sullivan, *op. cit.*, p. 48.

10. Quoted in Fritz Schmalenbach, *Jugendstil—ein Beitrag zu Theorie und Geschichte der Flächenkunst* (Würzburg, 1935), p. 28.

11. *Ibid.*

12. Pointillism's technique lends equivalence to figure and ground (or interstice).

13. Goya's sloping treatment of space and body rendered this reduction easier.

14. Selz and Constantine, *op. cit.*, p. 66.

15. Hoelzel paid particular attention to "intervallic figures" and "intervallic forms" ("Über Formen und Massenverteilung im Bilde," *Ver Sacrum*, XV [1901], 243).

16. Alois Riegl, *Die Spätrömische Kunstindustrie* (Vienna, 1929), p. 72.

17. Max Wertheimer, as quoted in Bruno Petermann, *Die Wertheimer-Koffka-Köhlerische Gestalttheorie und das Gestaltproblem* (Leipzig, 1929), p. 44.

18. E. Rubin, *Visuell wahrgenommene Figuren* (Copenhagen, 1921).

19. Kurt Koffka, *Principles of Gestalt Psychology* (New York, 1935), p. 71.

20. Henry van de Velde, "Ein Kapitel über Entwurf und Bau mod-

erner Möbel" (from *Pan*, 1897), in *Zum neuen Stil: Aus seinen Schriften ausgewählt und eingeleitet von Hans Curjel* (Munich, 1955), p. 60.

21. *Ibid.*, p. 59.

22. Frank Lloyd Wright, *A Testament* (New York, 1957), p. 224.

23. Henry-Russell Hitchcock, "Architecture," in Selz and Constantine, *op. cit.*, p. 123.

24. *Ibid.*, p. 60.

25. Quoted in Michel Seuphor, *Piet Mondrian: Life and Work* (New York, n.d.), p. 306.

26. Maurice Besset, *Gustave Eiffel* (Paris, 1957), *passim*.

27. The Fagus Works, incidentally, exemplifies an important characteristic of Cubism—the overlapping, polyvalent form complex (*Ill. 141*). The multistory glass walls overlap both the apertures and the horizontal bands separating them. Whereas in architecture the polyvalent form complex could ignore the limits set by functionalism, in contemporary Cubist painting it was able to impose its autonomy at the various levels of things. This is shown by Gris's *Still Life with Guitar* (1915, *Ill. 121*).

28. Seuphor, *op. cit.*, p. 118.

29. Selz and Constantine, *op. cit.*, p. 49.

30. *Ibid.*, p. 52.

31. Hans H. Hofstätter, "Symbolismus und Jugendstil im Frühwerk von Paul Klee," *Kunst in Hessen und am Mittelrhein*, V (Darmstadt, 1966), 97.

32. Liliane Brion-Guerry, *Cézanne et l'expression de l'espace* (Paris, 1966), p. 126; Meyer Schapiro, *Cézanne*, 2nd edition (New York, 1962), p. 98.

33. In his thorough study on Cézanne's spatial concepts, Fritz Novotny was the first to observe ambiguities of this kind in one of the views of L'Estaque (Venturi 399, 1883) (*Cézanne und das Ende der wissenschaftlichen Perspektive* [Vienna, 1938], p. 64).

34. Alfred Lichtwark, "Palastfenster und Flügeltür," *Pan* (Berlin, 1896), p. 57.

35. Arthur Rössler, as quoted by Selz and Constantine, *op. cit.*, p. 81.

36. Konrad Wachsmann, *Wendepunkt im Bauen* (Reinbek bei Hamburg, 1962), p. 74.

37. Greta Daniel, "Decorative Arts," in Selz and Constantine, *op. cit.*, p. 105.

38. Henri Bergson, "Matière et Mémoire," in *Oeuvres* (Paris, 1963), p. 324.

39. *Ibid.*, p. 333.

40. *Ibid.*, p. 332.

41. *Ibid.*, p. 334.

42. Werner Hofmann, *Grundlagen der Modernen Kunst* (Stuttgart, 1966), p. 229.

43. Bergson, "L'Evolution Créatrice," *op. cit.*, p. 711.

44. See note 5, above.

45. *Ibid.*, p. 714.

46. *Ibid.*, p. 716.

VI: CONCLUSIONS

1. Françoise Gilot and Carlton Lake, *Life with Picasso* (New York, 1964), pp. 75–76.

2. Marcel Duchamp, *Marchand du Sel* (Paris, 1958), p. 109.

3. Ernest Renan, *Saint-Paul* (Paris, n.d.), p. lxxvii.

4. This phrase is the title of Part IV in Jacob Burkhardt, *The Civilization of the Renaissance in Italy*, II (New York, 1958), p. 279.

5. Leonardo da Vinci, Ashburnham Ms., I, fol. 25r, in the Institute de France, Paris.

6. Werner Hofmann, *Grundlagen der Modernen Kunst* (Stuttgart, 1966), p. 463.

LIST OF ARTISTS

*The artists are arranged in alphabetical order. The numbers in italics
refer to the illustration number.*

ANONYMOUS. Entrance Door, Milan, 1899. *11.*

BALLA, GIACOMO. *Mercury Passing Before the Sun*, 1914. Collection
Gianni Mattioli, Milan. *52.*

BARTHOLOMÉ, PAUL ALBERT. *Monument to the Dead*, 1899. Père-
Lachaise Cemetery, Paris. *31.*

BEARDSLEY, AUBREY. *Singer*, c. 1898. From *The Poster* (London, I
[October 1898], 132). *152.*

BERLAGE, HENDRIK PETRUS. Amsterdam Stock Exchange, stairway, 1901.
Photo: Leonardo Benevolo, Rome. *135.*

BERNARD, ÉMILE. *Bathers*, 1889. Formerly collection Wildenstein, New
York. Photo: A. C. Cooper Ltd., London. *146.*

BOCCIONI, UMBERTO. *The Dream (Paolo and Francesca)*, 1908. Galleria
Blu, Milan. *44.*

Mob Gathered Around a Monument, 1908. Mrs. Barnett Malbin
(The Lydia and Harry Lewis Winston Collection) . Photo: Joseph
Klima, Jr., Detroit. *45.*

Development of a Bottle in Space, 1912. Collection, The Museum of
Modern Art, New York (Aristide Maillol Fund). *58.*

States of Mind I, The Farewells, 1911. Private collection, New York.
Photo: Charles Uht, New York. *118.*

BRANCUSI, CONSTANTIN. *The Kiss*, 1908. Philadelphia Museum of Art

[269]

(The Louise and Walter Arensberg Collection). Photo: A. J. Wyatt. *83.*

BRAQUE, GEORGES. *Countryside Near La Ciotat,* 1907. Galerie Louise Leiris, Paris. *93.*

Viaduct Near L'Estaque, 1907. Galerie Louise Leiris, Paris. *94.*

Still Life with Violin and Bowl, 1910. Kunstmuseum Basel. *96.*

CARRÀ, CARLO. *The Swimmers,* 1910. Museum of Art, Carnegie-Mellon University, Pittsburgh. *53.*

CÉZANNE, PAUL. *The Large Bathers,* 1898–1905. Philadelphia Museum of Art (The Wilstach Collection). Photo: A. J. Wyatt. *79.*

Foliage, 1895–1900. Collection, The Museum of Modern Art, New York (Lillie P. Bliss Collection). *95.*

Still Life with Plaster Cast, c. 1895. Courtauld Institute Gallery, London. *147.*

CHAGALL, MARC. *Half-Past Three,* 1911. Philadelphia Museum of Art (The Louise and Walter Arensberg Collection). Photo: A. J. Wyatt. *117.*

CRAIG, EDWARD GORDON. Stage design for *Hamlet,* project, 1908. Reproduced from Denise Bablet, *E.G.C.* (Paris: L'Arche Editeur, 1962). Photo: Meyer, Vienna. *69.*

CRANE, WALTER. "The Oval and the Rectangular Method," 1900. From Walter Crane, *Line and Form* (London, 1902 [1st edition, 1900]). *92.*

DE CHIRICO, GIORGIO. *The Philosopher's Conquest,* 1914. Courtesy of The Art Institute of Chicago (The Joseph Winterbotham Collection). *126.*

DELAUNAY, ROBERT. *Simultaneous Windows,* 1911. Hamburger Kunsthalle, Hamburg. Courtesy Mme. Sonja Delaunay. Photo: Ralph Kleinhempel, Hamburg. *111.*

The Team from Cardiff, 1913. Stedelijk van Abbemuseum, Eindhoven. Photo: Marmen Coppens, Eindhoven. *112.*

DERAIN, ANDRÉ. *Squatting Man,* 1907. Museum des 20. Jahrhunderts, Vienna. *80.*

DUCHAMP, MARCEL. *Bottle Rack* (Galerie Schwarz edition, 1964; original lost), 1914. Courtesy Cordier & Ekstrom, Inc., New York. Photo: Bacci, Milan, *104.*

Bicycle Wheel, 1913. Collection, The Museum of Modern Art, New York (The Sidney and Harriet Janis Collection, fractional gift). Photo: Geoffrey Clements, New York. *105.*

The Bride, 1912. Philadelphia Museum of Art (The Louise and Walter Arensberg Collection). *115.*

Sad Young Man in a Train, 1910–11. Peggy Guggenheim Foundation, Venice. *123.*

DUMONT, HENRI. *Tous les Soirs aux Ambassadeurs (Yvette Guilbert),* 1900. Collection, The Museum of Modern Art, New York. *154.*

ECKMANN, OTTO. Initial, c. 1900. Designed for the Rudhard Type Foundry, Offenbach. Reproduced from Robert Schmutzler, *Art Nouveau* (New York: Abrams, 1964) p. 212. *24.*

ENDELL, AUGUST. Atelier Elvira, facade (destroyed), Munich, 1897. Photo: Courtesy The Museum of Modern Art, New York. *12.*

FEININGER, LYONEL. *Umpferstedt I,* 1914. Kunstsammlung Nordrhein-Westfalen, Düsseldorf. Formerly in the collection of Andreas Feininger, courtesy of Mrs. Lyonel Feininger. Photo: Peter Witte, Spich über Troisdorf. *114.*

GALLÉ, ÉMILE. Shell-shaped crystal bowl, 1899. Kunstgewerbemuseum Zürich. *15.*

GALLEN, AXEL. Vignette, 1895. From *Pan.* Photo Meyer, Vienna. *43.*

GAUDÍ, ANTONIO. Casa Batlló, interior, Barcelona, 1905–07. Photo: Courtesy The Museum of Modern Art, New York. *14.*

Dressing table, 1885–89. Amigos de Gaudí, Palacio Güell, Barcelona. *132.*

GAUGUIN, PAUL. *Jacob Wrestling with the Angel (The Vision after the Sermon),* 1888. The National Gallery of Scotland, Edinburgh. *8.*

Personnages Comiques, 1889. From *Le Sourire.* Photo Meyer, Vienna. *89.*

Still Life with Three Puppies, 1888. Collection, The Museum of Modern Art, New York (Mrs. Simon Guggenheim Fund). *145.*

GERSTL, RICHARD. *The Arnold Schoenberg Family,* 1908. Private collection, Switzerland. *109.*

GRIS, JUAN. *Still Life with Guitar,* 1915. Rijksmuseum Kröller-Müller, Otterlo. *121.*

[271]

GROPIUS, WALTER, and ADOLF MEYER. Model Factory, Werkbund Exhibition, Cologne, 1914. Photo: Walter Gropius, Cambridge, Mass. *140.*

Fagus Works, Alfeld an der Leine, 1911–13. Walter Gropius with Adolf Meyer. Photo: Dr. Hans Hildebrandt, Stuttgart. *141.*

GUIMARD, HECTOR. Paris subway station (Métropolitain), entrance gate, c. 1900. Collection, The Museum of Modern Art, New York (Gift of Régie Autonome des Transports Parisiens). *10.*

Castel Henriette, Sèvres, 1903. Photo: Jacques Nestgen, Paris. *136.*

HAUSMANN, RAOUL. *The Spirit of Our Time (Mechanical Head),* 1920. Collection Raoul Hausmann. *125.*

HODLER, FERDINAND. *Night,* 1890. Kunstmuseum, Bern. Photo: H. Stebler, Bern. *40.*

HOFFMANN, JOSEF. Palais Stoclet, Brussels, 1905–11. Photo: Dr. Franz Stoedtner, Düsseldorf. *1.*

Palais Stoclet, dining room, Brussels, 1905–11. Foto Ritter, Vienna. *2.*

Supraporte (stucco relief from the 14th exhibition of the *Secession*), Vienna, 1902. Bildarchiv, Osterreichische Nationalbibliothek, Vienna. *18.*

Palais Stoclet, site plan, Brussels, 1905–11. Courtesy Eduard F. Sekler. Reproduced from *Moderne Bauformen,* Vol. 13 (1914). *51.*

Vase, before 1906. Landesgewerbeamt Baden Württemberg, Stuttgart. *142.*

HORTA, VICTOR. Hotel van Eetveld, hall, Brussels, 1895. Marburg-Art Reference Bureau, Ancram, New York. *16.*

Maison du Peuple (destroyed), facade, Brussels, 1897–99. Marburg-Art Reference Bureau, Ancram, New York. *138.*

KANDINSKY, WASSILY. Catalogue jacket, *Der Blaue Reiter,* 1911. Reproduced from Robert Schmutzler, *Art Nouveau* (New York, Abrams, 1964), p. 211. *27.*

Couple Riding, 1905–07. Städtische Galerie, Munich. *77.*

St. George III, 1911. Städtische Galerie, Munich. *78.*

Watercolor (first abstract watercolor), 1910. Collection Nina Kandinsky. Photo: Claude Gaspari, Galerie Maeght, Paris. *91.*

KIRCHNER, ERNST LUDWIG. *Man and Woman,* woodcut cycle, 1904. Copyright R. N. Ketterer, Campione d'Italia, Lugano. Photo Meyer, Vienna. *36.*

Streetwalkers by a Shop Window, c. 1913. Staatsgalerie, Stuttgart. Copyright R. N. Ketterer, Campione d'Italia, Lugano. *37.*

Drawings, in letter to Fritz Winter, May 3, 1929. R. N. Ketterer. *90.*

KIRCHNER, EUGEN. *November*, 1896. From *Pan* (II/3, 1896). Photo Meyer, Vienna. *23.*

KLEE, PAUL. *Two Fish, One Hook, One Worm*, 1901. Felix Klee Collection, Bern. *153.*

KLIMT, GUSTAV. *The Kiss (Realization)*, dining room frieze, Palais Stoclet, Brussels, 1905–08. Foto Ritter, Vienna. *6.*

Fischblut (Apathy), 1903. From *Ver Sacrum* (1903). Photo Meyer, Vienna. *54.*

Woods, c. 1900. Staatliche Kunstsammlungen (Gemäldegalerie Neue Meister), Dresden. Photo: Deutsche Fotothek Dresden. *62.*

KOKOSCHKA, OSKAR. *Dreaming Youths*, 1908. From *Wiener Werkstätte* (1908 edition). Courtesy Marlborough-Gerson Gallery. Photo: Fogg Art Museum, Cambridge, Mass. *38.*

The Wind's Bride (Tempest), 1914. Kunstmuseum Basel. *41.*

Murder Is the Hope of Women, 1908. Staatsgalerie, Stuttgart. Copyright Marlborough Fine Art Ltd. in Behalf of the Artist. *84.*

Self Portrait, c. 1908. Courtesy, Museum of Fine Arts, Boston (J. H. and E. A. Payne Fund). *85.*

KUPKA, FRANK. *The Black Idol*, 1900. Courtesy Mme. Kupka. *48.*

Vertical Planes in Blue and Red, 1913. Galerie Louis Carré, Paris. Courtesy Mme. Kupka. *68.*

Nocturne, 1911. Museum des 20. Jahrhunderts, Vienna. *71.*

Keyboard Landscape, 1909. Národní Galerie, Prague. Photo Meyer, Vienna. *72.*

Nocturne, 1900 (illustration for a poem by René Paux). Photo: Bibliothèque Nationale, Paris. *73.*

Amorpha, Fugue in Two Colors, 1912. Národní Galerie, Prague. *74.*

LARIONOV, MICHAEL. *Rain*, 1902. Courtesy Mme. Larionov. *63.*

Kourva Manja, 1907. Courtesy Mme. Larionov. Photo: Étienne Weill, Paris. *87.*

Blue Rayonism, 1912. Collection Boris Tcherkinsky, Paris. *120.*

Léger, Fernand. *Nudes in the Forest*, 1909/10. Rijksmuseum Kröller-Müller, Otterlo. *110.*

Loos, Adolf. Haberdashery Shop Goldman (destroyed), Vienna, 1898. Photoatelier Gerlach. *17.*

Steiner House, Vienna, 1910, three views. Photo: Heinrich Kulka, Vienna (101–02). Photoatelier Gerlach (103). *101, 102, 103.*

Mackintosh, Charles Rennie. Glasgow School of Art, library, interior, 1907–09. Crown Copyright, National Monuments Record. *100.*

Glasgow School of Art, north elevation, 1896. Courtesy Thomas Howarth, Toronto. *137.*

Willow Tea Room, Glasgow, 1904. Reproduced from Thomas Howarth, *Mackintosh* (New York: Wittenborn, 1953), plate 54. *143.*

Mackmurdo, Arthur Heygate. Title page for *Wren's City Churches*, 1883. Crown Copyright, Victoria and Albert Museum. *151.*

Maillol, Aristide. *Night*, c. 1902. Kunstmuseum Winterthur. Courtesy Dina Vierny, Paris. *82.*

Malevich, Kasimir. *Suprematism—18th Construction*, 1914. Stedelijk Museum, Amsterdam. *108.*

Marc, Franz. *Battling Forms*, 1914. Bayerische Staatsgemäldesammlungen, Munich. Courtesy Otto Stangl. *119.*

Martin, Camille. *See* Prouvé, Victor.

Matisse, Henri. *Woman with the Hat*, 1905. Collection Mr. and Mrs. Walter A. Haas, San Francisco. *3.*

Joie de Vivre, 1905–06. Copyright The Barnes Foundation, Merion Station, Pennsylvania. *7.*

The Red Studio, 1911. Collection, The Museum of Modern Art, New York (Mrs. Simon Guggenheim Fund). *21.*

Joie de Vivre, sketch, 1905. Collection Mr. and Mrs. Walter A. Haas, San Francisco. *35.*

Dance, c. 1910. The State Hermitage Museum, Leningrad. *81.*

Meyer, Adolf. *See* Gropius, Walter.

Minne, Georges. *Kneeling Youth*, c. 1898. Museum des 20. Jahrhunderts, Vienna. *39.*

Mondrian, Piet. *Composition in Oval (Composition in Blue, Grey and Pink)*, 1913–14. Loan, S. B. Slijper, Collection Haags Gemeentemuseum, The Hague. *59.*

Pier and Ocean, 1914. Collection, The Museum of Modern Art, New York (Mrs. Simon Guggenheim Fund). *60.*

Composition with Trees II, 1912–13. Loan, S. B. Slijper, Collection Haags Gemeentemuseum, The Hague. *64.*

Evolution (triptych), 1911. Loan, S. B. Slijper, Collection Haags Gemeentemuseum, The Hague. *65.*

Lighthouse at Westkapelle, 1908. S. B. Slijper, Collection Haags Gemeentemuseum, The Hague. *70.*

Composition in Blue, B, 1917. Rijksmuseum Kröller-Müller, Otterlo. *107.*

Drawing in a letter to James Johnson Sweeney, May 24, 1943. Courtesy James Johnson Sweeney. Photo: Solomon R. Guggenheim Museum, New York. *128.*

Perspective Géométrique, 1926. Reproduced from *Art d'Aujourd'hui* (April-May 1951). *129.*

MOSER, KOLOMAN. Desk and chair, 1904. Palais Stoclet, Brussels. Reproduced from Maurice Rheims, *The Flowering of Art Nouveau* (New York: Abrams, 1966), fig. 359. Photo: Studio Minders, Genk, Belgium. *133.*

MUNCH, EDVARD. *Funeral March*, 1897. Munch Museet, Oslo Kommunes Kunstsamlinger, Oslo. *26.*

The Cry, 1895. Munch Museet, Oslo Kommunes Kunstsamlinger, Oslo. *28.*

Portrait of Friedrich Nietzsche, 1906. Thielska Galleriet, Stockholm. *29.*

The Kiss, 1892. Munch Museet, Oslo Kommunes Kunstsamlinger, Oslo. *30.*

Meeting in Infinity (Encounter in Space), 1899. Munch Museet, Oslo Kommunes Kunstsamlinger, Oslo. *42.*

Menschenberg (Human Mountain), sketch, 1910. Munch Museet, Oslo Kommunes Kunstsamlinger, Oslo. *56.*

Woman (Sphinx), 1899. Courtesy of The Art Institute of Chicago (The Clarence Buckingham Collection). *66.*

NOLDE, EMIL. *Peasants*, 1908. Nolde Museum, Seebüll. Photo: Ralph Kleinhempel, Hamburg. *86.*

OBRIST, HERMANN. *Sketch for a Monument*, c. 1902. Copyright Kunstgewerbemuseum, Zürich. *55.*

Pillar (destroyed), 1898. Photo: courtesy Verlag Gerd Hatje, Stuttgart. *144*.

OUD, J. J. P. House de Vonk, lower hall, Noordwijkerhout, 1917. Courtesy Mrs. Annie Oud-Dinaux, Wassenaar. *130*.

PANKOK, BERNHARD. Drawing room, Munich, c. 1900. Stadtmuseum, Munich. Reproduced from Maurice Rheims, *The Flowering of Art Nouveau* (New York: Abrams, 1966), fig. 317. Photo: Studio Minders, Genk, Belgium. *13*.

PICABIA, FRANCIS. *I See Again in Memory My Dear Udnie*, 1913. Collection, The Museum of Modern Art (The New York Hillman Periodicals Fund). *116*.

PICASSO, PABLO. *The End of the Road (Redemption)*, c. 1898. Courtesy Thannhauser Foundation, New York. The Solomon R. Guggenheim Museum, New York. *22*.

La Vie, 1903. The Cleveland Museum of Art (Gift of Hanna Fund, 1945). *32*.

Les Demoiselles d'Avignon, 1907. Collection, The Museum of Modern Art, New York (acquired through the Lillie P. Bliss Bequest). *33*.

Les Demoiselles d'Avignon, studies, 1907. Kunstmuseum Basel. *34*.

Still Life with Collage, 1912. Musée des Arts Décoratifs, Paris (Collection Henri Laugier, Paris). Photo: courtesy Alfred Kröner Verlag, Stuttgart. *97*.

Still Life, 1914. Collection Lady Penrose, London. Photo: courtesy The Museum of Modern Art, New York. *106*.

PROUVÉ, VICTOR, and CAMILLE MARTIN. Bookbinding, 1893. Musée de l'École de Nancy. Photo: Gilbert Mangin, Nancy. *131*.

REDON, ODILON. *La Mort Verte*, after 1905. Collection Mrs. Bertram Smith, New York. *25*.

RIETVELD, GERRIT THOMAS. Chair, 1917. Museum des 20. Jahrhunderts, Vienna, *127*.

RODIN, AUGUSTE. *Monument to Balzac*, 1897. Collection, The Museum of Modern Art, New York (presented in memory of Curt Valentin by his friends). *46*.

ROUAULT, GEORGES. *M. et Mme. Poulot*, 1905. Collection Philippe Leclerq, Hem, France. Courtesy Mme. Rouault. Photo: Florin, Tourcoing. *4*.

Sant'Elia, Antonio. *"New City,"* study, 1914. Foto Ghizzoni, Como. *49.*

Lighthouse Tower, 1913. Foto Ghizzoni, Como. *50.*

Schmithals, Hans. *Composition,* c. 1900. Stadtmuseum, Munich. *76.*

Schwitters, Kurt. *Construction for Noble Ladies,* 1919. The Los Angeles County Museum of Art. *124.*

Selmersheim, Tony and Pierre. Settee and bookshelf, c. 1902. Reproduced from Maurice Rheims, *The Flowering of Art Nouveau* (New York: Abrams, 1962), fig. 284. *134.*

Severini, Gino. *Dynamic Hieroglyphic of the Bal Tabarin,* 1912. Collection, The Museum of Modern Art, New York (acquired through the Lillie P. Bliss Bequest). *57.*

Toorop, Jan. *The Three Brides,* 1893. Rijksmuseum Kröller-Müller, Otterlo. *67.*

Toulouse-Lautrec, Henri de. *Au Pied du Sinai,* book jacket, 1898. Bibliothèque Nationale, Paris. *47.*

Parody on Sacred Wood of Puvis de Chavannes, 1884. Philadelphia Museum of Art. *148.*

Van de Velde, Henry. *Sun at Ocean (Rhythmic Synthesis),* c. 1888–89. Collection Hans Curjel, Zurich. Photo: Walter Dräyer, Zurich. *61.*

Abstract Composition, c. 1890. Rijksmuseum Kröller-Müller, Otterlo. *75.*

Title page from *Van Nu en Straks,* 1893. Reproduced from Robert Schmutzler, *Art Nouveau* (New York: Abrams, 1964), p. 16. *150.*

Belt buckle, c. 1898. Kunstgewerbemuseum Zürich. *155.*

Van Gogh, Vincent. *Starry Night,* 1889. Collection, The Museum of Modern Art, New York (acquired through the Lillie P. Bliss Bequest). *9.*

Villon, Jacques. *Soldiers on March,* 1913. Galerie Louis Carré, Paris. *113.*

Vlaminck, Maurice. *La Partie de Campagne,* 1905. Private collection, Paris. *5.*

Sur le Zinc (At the Bar), 1900. Musée Calvet, Avignon. *88.*

Wagner, Otto. Postal Savings Bank, interior, Vienna, 1904–06. Photo: Bildarchiv Österreichische Nationalbibliothek, Vienna. *20.*

[277]

Hofpavilion (Hietzing Station of the Vienna Underground), 1898. Photo Meyer, Vienna. *149.*

WRIGHT, FRANK LLOYD. Unity Church, ceiling detail, Oak Park, Illinois, 1906. Photo: Dr. Otto A. Graf, Vienna. *19.*

Unity Church, Oak Park, Illinois, 1906. Photo: courtesy The Museum of Modern Art, New York. *98.*

Office armchair, 1904. Collection, The Museum of Modern Art, New York (gift of Edgar Kaufmann, Jr.). *99.*

Winslow House, River Forest, Illinois, 1893. Reproduced from *Architectural Review*, VII (1900), plate XXXVI. *139.*

Addendum:

CARRÀ, CARLO. *The Daughters of Loth*, 1919. E. Bestagini, Milan. Photo: Galleria Gissi, Turin. *122.*

～ *INDEX*

A-B-C Art, 11, 238

Abstract Art, 23–24, 45, 47–48, 65–66, 68, 111, 134, 233, 235, 239

Allard, Roger, 130

Apollinaire, Guillaume, 79, 131, 136, 140, 162

Armory Show, 133, 171

Arp, Hans (Jean) (b. 1887), 172, 174

Art de synthèse, 20–23

Art Nouveau, 22, 28–29, 45, 47–48, 66–68, 74–75, 198–199, 207, 223, 228–229, 233–235

Aurier, Albert, 11, 21

Bacon, Francis, 202

Baldung-Grien, Hans, 134

Ball, Hugo, 135, 172

Balla, Giacomo (1871–1958)
Mercury Passing Before the Sun, 42, 131; *Ill.* 52

Barr, Alfred H., Jr., 19

Bartholomé, Paul Albert (1848–1928), 32, 43
Monument to the Dead, 32, 43; *Ill.* 31

Bauhaus, 136, 239

Beardsley, Aubrey (1872–1898), 202
Singer, 202; *Ill.* 152

Bellori, Giovanni Pietro, 174

Bergson, Henri, 41, 228–230, 237

Berlage, Hendrik Petrus (1856–1934), 200
Amsterdam Stock Exchange, stairway, 200; *Ill.* 135

Bernard, Émile (1868–1941), 78, 222
Bathers, 222; *Ill.* 146

Blake, William (1757–1827), 38

Blanc, Charles, 46

Blaue Reiter, Der, 66, 105, 130, 133–134

Bleyl, Fritz, 111

Boccioni, Umberto (1882–1916), 23, 38–39, 42, 136, 140
Development of a Bottle in Space, 42; *Ill.* 58
Mob Gathered Around a Monument, 39; *Ill.* 45
States of Mind I, The Farewells, 130; *Ill.* 118
The Dream (Paolo and Francesca), 38; *Ill.* 44

Bonnard, Pierre (1867–1947), 197
Dressing Gown, 197

Brancusi, Constantin (1876–1957), 73
The Kiss, 73; *Ill.* 83

Braque, Georges (1882–1963), 23, 77–78, 103–104, 130–131, 161
Countryside Near La Ciotat, 77; *Ill.* 93

Braque, Georges (*Cont.*)
  Still Life with Violin and Bowl, 34,
    80; *Ill*. 96
  Viaduct Near L'Estaque, 77–78; *Ill*.
    94
Brion-Guerry, Liliane, 223
Brücke, Die, 36, 43, 111
Burckhardt, Jacob, 236

Cabaret Voltaire, 135
Café Volpini Exhibition, 72
Camus, Albert, 166
Caravaggio, Michelangelo, 174
Carrà, Carlo (1881–1966), 42
  The Daughters of Loth, 134; *Ill*.
    122
  The Swimmers, 42; *Ill*. 53
Cézanne, Paul (1839–1906), 12, 71–72,
  78–79, 223, 234–236
  Foliage, 78–79; *Ill*. 95
  Still Life with Plaster Cast, 223;
    Ill. 147
  The Large Bathers, 72; *Ill*. 79
Cézanne Memorial Exhibition, 78
Chagall, Marc (b. 1889), 129–130
  Half-Past Three, 130; *Ill*. 117
Cloisonnism, 21, 27, 31, 33, 36–37,
  66–67, 73, 203
Constructivism, 11, 23, 136, 228, 233,
  238–239
Contamin, Victor (1840–1893), 208
  Halle des Machines, 208
Craig, Edward Gordon (1872–1966),
  48
  Stage design for *Hamlet*, 48; *Ill*. 69
Crane, Walter (1845–1915), 22, 76–79
  "The Oval and the Rectangular
    Method," 76; *Ill*. 92
Cubism, 13, 23–24, 33–34, 42, 48, 67–
  68, 71, 75, 77–80, 102–108, 111–
  112, 129–135, 137, 139–140, 143–
  144, 162–164, 167, 173, 196, 198–
  199, 207, 225, 234–236

Dadaism, 11, 13, 101, 135–136, 143,
  172–176, 196, 225, 228, 233, 236,
  238–239

D'Annunzio, Gabriele, 31
Dante Alighieri, 38, 43
De Chirico, Giorgio (b. 1888), 169–
  170
  The Philosopher's Conquest, 169;
    Ill. 126
Dehmel, Richard, 38
Delacroix, Eugène (1798–1863), 11–12,
  38
  Death of Sardanapalus, 38
Delaunay, Robert (1885–1941), 112,
  129–131
  Simultaneous Windows, 112, 130;
    Ill. 111
  The Team from Cardiff, 130; *Ill*.
    112
Denis, Maurice (1870–1943), 45, 67,
  112, 140, 206, 222, 229, 238
De Quincy, Quatremère, 11
Derain, André (1880–1954), 18, 72–73,
  77
  Squatting Man, 72–73; *Ill*. 80
De Staël, Nicolas (1914–1955), 13
De Stijl, 11, 13, 136, 141, 144, 163–
  164, 166–167, 170, 196, 236, 238
De Stijl, 135
Divisionism, 20, 27
Dresden Art Exhibition, 65
Duchamp, Marcel (1887–1968), 102,
  108, 129–130, 135–137, 141–143,
  161, 167–174, 201–202, 227, 233,
  235–236
  Bicycle Wheel, 102, 108; *Ill*. 105
  Bottle Rack, 102, 108, 141, 171;
    Ill. 104
  Nude Descending a Staircase, 171
  Sad Young Man in a Train, 137;
    Ill. 123
  The Bride, 130; *Ill*. 115
  Urinal, 171
Dujardin, Edouard, 21
Dumont, Henri
  Tous les Soirs aux Ambassadeurs,
    224; *Ill*. 154
Dutert, Ferdinand (1845–1906), 208
  Halle des Machines, 208

Eckmann, Otto (1865–1902), 31
Initial, 22, 31; *Ill.* 24
Ehrenfels, Christian von, 205, 207
Eiffel, Gustave (1832–1923), 208
Tower, 208
El Greco, 72, 134
Endell, August (1871–1925), 65, 226
Atelier Elvira, facade, 22, 226;
Ill. 12
Entrance Door, Milan, 22; *Ill.* 11
Erster Deutsche Herbstsalon (First
German Autumn Salon), 133–134
Exhibition of Independent Painters,
171
Expressionism, 23–24, 34–37, 68, 71,
74–75, 101, 106, 111, 134, 173,
234

Fauvism, 18, 20–21, 23, 66–67, 76–77,
79, 111–112, 134, 234
Feininger, Lyonel (1871–1956), 130
Umpferstedt I, 130; *Ill.* 114
Fénéon, Felix, 20
Fiedler, Conrad, 229
Fin de siècle, 18, 23–24, 38, 71, 196,
235
Focillon, Henri, 239
Friesz, Othon (1879–1949), 18
Futurism, 23–24, 39, 41–42, 67–68,
101, 130–131, 134–135, 173, 196,
228

Gallé, Émile (1846–1904)
Shell-shaped crystal bowl, 22; *Ill.*
15
Gallen, Axel (1865–1931), 38
Vignette, 38; *Ill.* 43
Gaudí, Antonio (1852–1926), 199–200,
226, 234–235
Casa Battló, interior, 22; *Ill.* 14
Dressing table, 200; *Ill.* 132
Gauguin, Paul (1848–1903), 12, 20–23,
27, 30–31, 33, 44–46, 48, 66, 71–
74, 79, 112, 197, 204, 222, 234–
236
Jacob Wrestling with the Angel

(The Vision after the Sermon),
20–21, 30–31, 72, 197; *Ill.* 8
Personnages Comiques, 74; *Ill.* 89
Soyez Amoreuses, 72
Still Life with Three Puppies, 222;
Ill. 145
The Yellow Christ, 72
*Vineyard in Arles with Breton
Women*, 72
*Where Do We Come From? What
Are We? Where Are We Going?*,
33
Gerstl, Richard, 111
The Arnold Schoenberg Family,
111; *Ill.* 109
Giedion-Welcker, Carola, 10
Gilot, Françoise, 74
Giotto, 238
Goya, Francisco, 204
Greenberg, Clement, 9–11
Gris, Juan (1887–1927), 131–133, 168,
200
Still Life with Guitar, 132, 200;
Ill. 121
Gropius, Walter (b. 1883), 208
Fagus Works, 264n; *Ill.* 141
Model Factory, 208; *Ill.* 140
Guimard, Hector (1867–1942), 224
Castel Henriette, 224; *Ill.* 136
Paris subway station, entrance gate,
22; *Ill.* 10

Hausmann, Raoul (b. 1886), 172
*The Spirit of Our Time
(Mechanical Head)*, 137, 172; *Ill.*
125
Heckel, Erich (b. 1883), 111
Hegel, Georg W. F., 12, 171
Henry, Charles, 32, 46
Hodler, Ferdinand (1853–1918), 32–
33, 38, 46–47, 205
Night, 32, 38; *Ill.* 40
Hoelzel, Adolf (1853–1934), 205
Hoffmann, Josef (1870–1955), 17–18,
28, 36, 40, 48, 71, 98, 100, 226
Palais Stoclet, 17, 39, 226; *Ill.* 1

Hoffman, Josef (*Cont.*)
  Palais Stoclet, dining room, 17;
    Ill. 2
  Palais Stoclet, site plan, 40; *Ill.*
    51
  Supraporte, 23, 48, 98; *Ill.* 18
  Vase, 226; *Ill.* 142
Hofmann, Julius von, 197
  Idyllic Landscape with Bathers, 197
Hokusai, 30
Horace, 80
Horta, Victor (1861–1947), 200, 226,
  235
  Hotel van Eetveld, hall, 22; *Ill.* 16
  Maison du Peuple, facade, 200; *Ill.*
    138
Huelsenbeck, Richard, 172
Huszar, Vilmos, 163

Impressionism, 20–21
Ingres, Jean-Auguste Dominique
  (1780–1867), 134

Janco, Marcel (b. 1895), 172–173
Jawlensky, Alexei von (1864–1941),
  111
Journal de Rouen, 18
Jugendstil, 11, 13, 22, 24, 34–36, 38,
  40–42, 44–45, 48, 65–67, 74, 76,
  79, 97, 99, 101, 106, 144, 165–
  167, 174–175, 196, 198–199, 202,
  204, 206–208, 222, 224–227, 229–
  230, 234–235

Kahnweiler, Daniel-Henry, 78–79,
  104–105, 132–133, 143, 167
Kandinsky, Wassily (1866–1944), 23,
  27, 31, 45, 65–67, 71, 75, 105,
  107–108, 111–113, 135–143,
  169–170, 197–198, 201, 208, 222,
  225, 227, 230, 234–237, 239
  Catalogue jacket, *Der Blaue Reiter*,
    31; *Ill.* 27
  Couple Riding, 65; *Ill.* 77
  St. George III, 66; *Ill.* 78
  Watercolor, 75, 112, 234; *Ill.* 91

Keats, John, 97
Kirchner, Ernst Ludwig (1880–1938),
  23, 35–36, 39, 45, 67, 74–75, 111
  Drawings, 74; *Ill.* 90
  Man and Woman, 35–36, 39, 45,
    74; *Ill.* 36
  Streetwalkers by a Shop Window,
    35; *Ill.* 37
Kirchner, Eugen, 31
  November, 31; *Ill.* 23
Klee, Paul (1879–1940), 222
  Two Fish, One Hook, One Worm,
    222–223; *Ill.* 153
Klimt, Gustav (1862–1918), 18–19, 21–
  22, 24, 32–33, 36, 38, 42, 46, 65,
  197–199, 233
  Beethoven frieze, 197
  Eternal Spring, 38
  Fischblut (Apathy), 42; *Ill.* 54
  Medicine, 32
  The Dead, 32
  The Kiss (Realization), 18–19, 24,
    33, 197; *Ill.* 6
  Woods, 46; *Ill.* 62
Klinger, Max (1857–1920), 35, 197
  Amor and Psyche, 35
  Judgment of Paris, 197
Kok, Antonie, 163
Kokoschka, Oskar (b. 1886), 23, 35–
  38, 67, 71, 73, 101, 111, 134
  Dreaming Youths, 36–37, 73; *Ill.* 38
  Murder Is the Hope of Women, 73;
    Ill. 84
  Self Portrait, 37, 73; *Ill.* 85
  The Wind's Bride (Tempest), 37–
    38, 134; *Ill.* 41
Kubin, Alfred (1877–1959), 137
Kunstschau Exhibition, 111
Kupka, Frank (1871–1957), 23, 39, 45–
  46, 48, 65, 67, 112
  Amorpha, Fugue in Two Colors,
    65, 112; *Ill.* 74
  Keyboard Landscape, 48; *Ill.* 72
  Nocturne, 48; *Ill.* 71
  Nocturne, 46, 48; *Ill.* 73
  The Black Idol, 39; *Ill.* 48

Vertical Planes in Blue and Red, 48; *Ill.* 68

Lacombe, Georges (1868–1916), 33
Birth of Man, 33
The Death of Man, 33
The Dream, 33
The Uniting, 33
Laforgue, Jules, 174
Larionov, Michael (1881–1964), 46, 74, 101, 112, 131, 135
Blue Rayonism, 112, 131; *Ill.* 120
Kourva Manja, 74; *Ill.* 87
Rain, 46; *Ill.* 63
League of Youth, 135
Léger, Fernand (1881–1955), 129–131
Nudes in the Forest, 130; *Ill.* 110
Leonardo da Vinci, 173, 237
Mona Lisa, 173
Le Roy, Madame, 172
Lichtwark, Alfred, 224
Loos, Adolf (1870–1933), 46, 71, 98–104
Haberdashery Shop Goldman, 23, 98; *Ill.* 17
Steiner House, 103–104; *Ills.* 101–103

Mackintosh, Charles Rennie (1868–1928), 71, 98, 198, 200, 226, 234
Glasgow School of Art, library, 98, 226; *Ill.* 100
Glasgow School of Art, north elevation, 200; *Ill.* 137
Willow Tea Room, 226; *Ill.* 143
Mackmurdo, Arthur Heygate (1851–1942), 23, 226
Title page for *Wren's City Churches*, 23, 226; *Ill.* 151
Mahler, Alma, 37
Maillol, Aristide (1861–1944), 73
Night, 73; *Ill.* 82
Malevich, Kasimir (1878–1935), 141
Suprematism—18th Construction, 256n; *Ill.* 108
Man Ray (b. 1890), 173

Marc, Franz (1880–1916), 66, 130–131, 135, 143
Battling Forms, 131; *Ill.* 119
Marinetti, Filippo Tommaso (1876–1944), 41–42
Martin, Camille
Bookbinding, 198; *Ill.* 131
Marx, Karl, 164
Matisse, Henri (1869–1954), 18–21, 23–24, 27–29, 37, 40, 65, 67, 71–73, 75–77, 111–112, 197, 222, 233, 235–236
Dance, 73; *Ill.* 81
Joie de Vivre, 18–19, 27–30, 37, 65, 72, 75, 77, 197, 202–204, 222; *Ill.* 7
Joie de Vivre, sketch, 76; *Ill.* 35
The Red Studio, 28–29, 67, 76, 197; *Ill.* 21
Woman with the Hat, 18, 24; *Ill.* 3
Matthies, Carl, 204
MERZ pictures, 139–140
Meyer, Adolf (1840–1911), 208
Fagus Works, 264n; *Ill.* 141
Model Factory, 208; *Ill.* 140
Minne, Georges (1866–1941), 36
Kneeling Youth, 36; *Ill.* 39
Mondrian, Piet (1872–1944), 23, 45–48, 66–67, 71, 75, 80, 102, 108, 112, 129, 135–138, 142–144, 161–168, 170–171, 196, 207–208, 225, 233–236
Composition in Blue, B., 108; *Ill.* 107
Composition in Oval (Composition in Blue, Grey and Pink), 46, 48, 234; *Ill.* 59
Composition with Trees II, 137, 144; *Ill.* 64
Drawing, 144; *Ill.* 128
Evolution, 47; *Ill.* 65
Lighthouse at Westkapelle, 46; *Ill.* 70
Perspective Géométrique, 161; *Ill.* 129

[283]

Mondrian, Piet (*Cont.*)
  Pier and Ocean, 46, 112, 138; *Ill.*
    60
Morris, William (1834–1896), 144, 167
Moser, Koloman (1868–1916), 17, 224,
    226
  Desk and chair, 224, 226; *Ill.* 133
Munch, Edvard (1863–1944), 28, 32–
    33, 38, 43–44, 47, 234
  Funeral March, 43; *Ill.* 26
  Harpy, 32
  *Meeting in Infinity (Encounter in
    Space*, 38; *Ill.* 42
  Menschenberg (Human Mountain),
    sketch, 43–44; *Ill.* 56
  Portrait of Friedrich Nietzsche, 32;
    Ill. 29
  The Cry, 32; *Ill.* 28
  The Dance of Life, 47
  The Kiss, 33; *Ill.* 30
  Woman (Sphinx), 47; *Ill.* 66
Münter, Gabriele, 111

Neo-Dadaism, 11
Neo-Impressionism, 65
Neo-Plasticism, 163, 165
Neue Künstlervereinigung (New
    Artists' Union), 111
Nietzsche, Friedrich, 39, 41, 43, 80,
    102, 143, 205
Nolde, Emil (1867–1956), 73, 204
  Peasants, 73; *Ill.* 86
Nouveau Réalisme, 11

Obrist, Hermann (1863–1927), 42–43,
    65, 228
  Pillar, 228; *Ill.* 144
  Sketch for a Monument, 42; *Ill.* 55
Olbrich, Josef Maria (1867–1908), 98,
    100–101, 200
Op Art, 11, 238
Orphism, 131
Oud, J. J. P. (1890–1963), 163–164
  House de Vonk, lower hall, 164;
    Ill. 130

Pan, 198
Pankok, Bernhard (1872–1943)
  Drawing room, 22; *Ill.* 13
Paxton, Joseph (1801–1865), 208
  Crystal Palace, 208
Picabia, Francis (1878–1953), 129–130,
    171–172
  *I See Again in Memory My Dear
    Udnie*, 130; *Ill.* 116
Picasso, Pablo (b. 1881), 23, 31–34,
    36, 43, 67, 72–78, 101, 103, 130–
    131, 133–134, 161, 197, 234–235
  La Vie, 33–34, 73, 197; *Ill.* 32
  Les Demoiselles d'Avignon, 33–34,
    67, 72–73, 78; *Ill.* 33
  Les Demoiselles d'Avignon, studies,
    34, 76; *Ill.* 34
  Still Life, 136; *Ill.* 106
  Still Life with Collage, 33–34, 104,
    133, 198–199; *Ill.* 97
  The End of the Road (Redemption),
    31–33, 43; *Ill.* 22
Pisanello, Antonio, 45
Pointilism, 27
Pollock, Jackson (1912–1956), 10
Pop Art, 11, 238
Prouvé, Victor (1858–1943)
  Bookbinding, 198; *Ill.* 131

Raphael, 11
Rayonism, 131, 135
Redon, Odilon (1840–1916), 31–32,
    195, 204, 222, 225
  Death, 32
  La Mort Verte, 31; *Ill.* 25
Renan, Ernest, 236
Reynolds, Sir Joshua, 63, 135
Richter, Hans (b. 1888), 172, 174
Riegl, Alois, 106–108, 205
Riemerschmid, Richard (1868–1957),
    234
Rietveld, Gerrit Thomas (1888–1964),
    141, 163–164, 167
  Chair, 141; *Ill.* 127
Rilke, Rainer Maria, 43

Rodin, Auguste (1840–1917), 32, 38–
  39, 43–44, 73
  Amor and Psyche, 38
  Monument to Balzac, 39; *Ill.* 46
  The Gates of Hell, 32, 43
  The Thinker, 39
  Tower of Work, 43–44
Rouault, Georges (1871–1958), 18, 74,
  101
  M. et Mme. Poulot, 18, 74; *Ill.* 4
Runge, Philipp Otto (1777–1810), 12
Ruskin, John, 97, 100, 144, 167, 174
Russolo, Luigi (1885–1947), 173

Salon d'Automne, 18, 72, 74, 77–78
Salon des Indépendants, 27
Sant'Elia, Antonio (1888–1916), 39–40
  Lighthouse Tower, 40; *Ill.* 50
  "New City," study, 40; *Ill.* 49
Schapiro, Meyer, 223
Scheffler, Karl, 204
Schmidt-Rottluff, Karl (b. 1884), 111
Schmithals, Hans (b. 1878), 65
  Composition, 65; *Ill.* 76
Schoenberg, Arnold, 38, 111
Schopenhauer, Arthur, 169–170
Schuffenecker, Émile, 44
Schwitters, Kurt (1887–1948), 139–140
  Construction for Noble Ladies, 137,
  140; *Ill.* 124
Selmersheim, Pierre and Tony
  Settee and bookshelf, 226; *Ill.* 134
Selz, Peter, 197, 205
Seurat, Georges (1859–1891), 204
Severini, Gino (1883–1966), 163
  *Dynamic Hieroglyphic of the Bal
  Tabarin*, 42, 130; *Ill.* 57
Signac, Paul (1863–1935), 27, 203
Sonderbund Exhibition, 133
Soulages, Pierre (b. 1919), 12
Stamp, Percy, 226
Stoclet, Adolphe, 17
Sullivan, Louis H. (1850–1924), 97–98,
  195, 202, 204, 222, 225, 228
Surrealism, 136–137, 228, 239

Sweeney, James Johnson, 144
Symbolism, 22, 24, 32–33, 36–37, 45,
  47, 66–67, 174, 198
Synthetism, 112

Tiffany, Louis C. (1848–1933), 228,
  234–235
Tintoretto, Jacopo, 134
Tobey, Mark (b. 1890), 10
Toorop, Jan (1858–1928), 47
  The Three Brides, 47; *Ill.* 67
Toulouse-Lautrec, Henri de (1864–
  1901), 28, 39, 197
  Au Pied du Sinai, 39; *Ill.* 47
  *Parody on Sacred Wood of Puvis de
  Chavannes*, 197; *Ill.* 148
Townsend, Charles Harrison (1850–
  1928), 200
  Whitechapel Gallery, facade, 200
Tzara, Tristan, 172

Van der Leck, Bart (1876–1958), 163
Van de Velde, Henry (1863–1957), 11,
  28, 30–31, 36, 40–41, 44, 46, 48,
  65, 80, 99, 106, 161, 166–167,
  206–207, 224, 226, 228–229, 235
  Abstract Composition, 65, 234; *Ill.*
  75
  Belt buckle, 226; *Ill.* 155
  Sun at Ocean (Rhythmic Synthesis),
  46; *Ill.* 61
  Title page from *Van Nu en Straks*,
  224; *Ill.* 150
Van Doesburg, Theo (1883–1931),
  163–164, 167, 196
Van Gogh, Vincent (1853–1890), 12,
  20–21, 23, 37–38, 71, 73, 79, 131,
  234–235
  Starry Night, 20–21, 37–38, 131;
  Ill. 9
Van't Hoff, Robert (1852–1911), 163
Vantongerloo, Georges (1886–1965),
  163
Viennese Secession, 17, 39–40, 98,
  100, 205

Villon, Jacques (1894–1963), 129–130
  Soldiers on March, 130; *Ill.* 113
Vlaminck, Maurice (1876–1958), 18, 74
  La Partie de Campagne, 18; *Ill.* 5
  Sur le Zinc (At the Bar), 74; *Ill.* 88

Wachsmann, Konrad, 227
Walden, Herworth, 133
Wagner, Otto (1841–1918), 39, 71, 98,
  223
  Hofpavilion, 223; *Ill.* 149
  Postal Savings Bank, interior, 23,
    98; *Ill.* 20

Wiener **Werkstätte, 17, 36**
Wils, Jan, 163
Wölfflin, Heinrich, 44–45
Worringer, Wilhelm, 105–107, 134,
  143–144
Wright, Frank Lloyd (1867–1959), 71,
  97–98, 206–207, 223
  Office armchair, 98; *Ill.* 99
  Unity Church, 97–98; *Ill.* 98
  Unity Church, ceiling detail, 23,
    97–98; *Ill.* 19
  Winslow House, 207, 224; *Ill.* 139